# Programming
# Lang5

Bernd Ulmann

**Autor:**
Prof. Dr. Bernd Ulmann
Schwalbacher Strasse 31
65307 Bad Schwalbach
Germany
ulmann@vaxman.de

.

ISBN-13: 978-1523448111
ISBN-10: 1523448113
Verantwortlich: Bernd Ulmann, Schwalbacher Strasse 31, 65307 Bad Schwalbach
Printed in Germany by Amazon Distribution GmbH, Leipzig

Gesetzt mit LaTeX.

To my beloved wife Rikka.

To my beloved wife Rikka.

# Acknowledgments

This book would not have been possible without the support and help of many people. First of all, I would like to thank my wife RIKKA MITSAM who never complained about the many hours I spent writing Lang5-code instead of being with her. In addition to that she did a lot of proofreading.

I am also greatly indebted to THOMAS KRATZ who did most of the implementation of the Lang5-interpreter and the Array::DeepUtils module. Without him there would be no Lang5-interpreter at all!

In addition to that, I would like to thank PATRICK HEDFELD for countless fruitful discussions about natural languages as well as programming languages and Lang5 in particular. He also did a terrific job writing the Lang5-Redbook.

MALCOLM BLUNDEN made many invaluable corrections and improvements to this text. He and BIANCA BRUNNER did a terrific job proofreading this book.

# Contents

# Chapter 1

# Introduction

## 1.1 Motivation

Over the last about 70 years more than 8,500 programming languages have been developed, most of which are long since forgotten. This book describes yet another programming language – one which fills a niche as it is stack-oriented like Forth and features $n$-dimensional arrays as its basic data structures like APL or J.

The particular language described in detail in this book is called Lang5 and has been developed explicitly to serve as an example to be used in an introductory lecture on programming languages and interpreter design.

All of the source code used and described in the following is available for free at http://lang5.sourceforge.net and should be downloaded and installed on a computer running LINUX, Mac OS X, Windows or even OpenVMS, since the remainder of this book makes heavy use of the interpreter, and solving the exercises requires a Lang5-interpreter at hand. The only prerequisite for running Lang5 is a Perl-interpreter since the Lang5-interpreter is written in Perl.

Accordingly, some programming experience, ideally with the Perl programming language, and a basic understanding of nested data structures built from arrays and hashes is a helpful prerequisite for reading this book which is not an introductory text about programming and data structures as such.

1

## 1.2   Array languages

First of all, what is a so-called *array language*? Most actively
used programming languages, some of which even became
part of our everyday vocabulary, like C, its derivatives C++ and
C#, Java, Perl, Python etc. are either *imperative*[1] or *object oriented* languages as the "TIOBE Programming Community Index for April 2013", shows: The ten most used programming
languages are either imperative (C being the most widely used
language) or object oriented languages.[2]

Languages employing other programming paradigms like
so-called *functional* or *array languages* are, unfortunately, used
only rarely according to TIOBE. LISP, for example, is on position 29 while APL, the archetypal array programming language, is not even listed on TIOBE in 2015.

This is a pity since both of these paradigms offer methods
and chances for programming that exceed those of the more
traditional languages taking up the first ranks. Especially array programming languages are highly powerful and yet extremely underestimated.

The idea of array languages is an old one: In the late 1950s,
KEN IVERSON, a mathematician who was not satisfied with the
traditional form of mathematical notation, set out to develop a
new notation when he was an assistant professor at Harvard.[3]
In 1960 KEN IVERSON began working for IBM where he met
ADIN FALKOFF who became interested in this new notation. He
extended his notation to a degree which made it possible to be
used for the description of algorithms and computer systems
in general.[4]

Internally, this language was known as *Iverson's Better Math*
but IBM did not like that name for obvious reasons, thus a
new name was needed. Finally, this extraordinary and sem-
inal language was named APL, short for *A Programming Language*. This name was used officially for the first time in the

---

[1] Also called VON NEUMANN *languages*.

[2] In December 2015, the top ten programming languages listed by
TIOBE (see http://www.tiobe.com/index.php/content/paperinfo/tpci/
index.html) were Java, C, C++, Python, C#, PHP, Visual Basic .NET,
JavaScript, Perl, and Ruby.

[3] See [JANKO 1980].

[4] The most famous example for a computer system description in this notation is that of the IBM /360 architecture in 1964 which is described in
[FALKOFF et al. 1964].

title of [IVERSON 1962] where it was still used as a method for *"interpersonal communication"*.[5]

The first noteworthy aspect of APL is its unusual character set which was (and often still is) considered a major obstacle as the following question asked by R. A. BROOKER shows:[6]

> *"Why do you insist on using a notation which is a nightmare for typist and compositor?"*

This question was even more important back in the early 1960s since there were no graphic displays capable of displaying the special APL characters available. IBM overcame this problem with the introduction of the so-called *Selectric Typewriter* which could use special character balls containing the characters required for the APL system. Despite this particular nuisance, the extreme consistency and efficiency of APL quickly led to the development of interpreters for this language.[7]

APL encourages a unique style of programming. On a first glance APL programs are quite unreadable for the uninitiated but as soon as one gets used to its special character set and its basic ideas, it turns out to be one of the most powerful programming languages ever. Especially its array features which make APL a so-called *array language* lead to unusual and often astonishingly short solutions for given problems compared with other programming languages.[8]

APL in its very nature is an interpreter language with an unusually high degree of interactivity for the time of its inception. It features dynamic typing, a property also found in today's *dynamic languages* like Perl, Python etc., but its main feature is its use of the vector as its basic data structure. Because of this, APL programs rely on vector and matrix operations and seldom use (explicit) loops, conditional execution and the like.

---

[5]See [JANKO 1980][p. 1].

[6]See [McDONNEL 1981][p. 11].

[7]HELLERMANN implemented an interpreter supporting a subset of APL on the IBM 1620 in 1963; an APL system running in batch mode was developed for the IBM 7090 mainframe in 1965 by M. L. BREED and P. S. ABRAMS who also implemented an APL system running under an experimental time sharing system on an IBM 7090 (see [JANKO 1980][p. 1]).

[8]This is, by the way, a good example of how notation and languages shape the way of problem description and solving. Ken Iverson's famous publication [IVERSON 1963] is a must read in this context.

The following example gives an impression of the power resulting from using vectors as basic data structures: The sum

$$\sum_{i=1}^{100} i$$

is to be computed. Using a typical imperative language like C this could be accomplished as follows:

```
 1    #include <stdio.h>
 2
 3    int main()
 4    {
 5        int sum, i;
 6
 7        for (i = sum = 0; i <= 100; sum += i++);
 8
 9        printf("%d\n", sum);
10        return 0;
11    }
```

As straightforward as such a solution may seem, only a small portion of this program (a single line, in fact) deals with the actual problem of computing the sum of all natural numbers $\leq 100$. The remaining lines deal with variable declaration, printing the result and terminating the program graciously – tasks which are not at all connected to the underlying problem to be solved. A typical APL solution of the same problem might look like this: $\boxed{+/\iota 100}$

It should be noted that APL statements are read from right to left, so this program applies the $\iota$ (*iota*) function to the scalar 100 which yields a vector with unit stride containing 100 elements. The next part is tricky: Using the reduction operator /, the dyadic operator + is applied between each two successive elements of this vector thus yielding $1+2+3+\ldots+99+100$. This is a typical idiom of an array language saving many of the explicit loops required by other, more traditional programming languages.

The next (and last) APL example[9] is more complicated but shows even more of the power of array languages in general. A

---

[9]Much more detailed information about APL can be found in [IVERSON 1962], [GILMAN et al. 1970], [IVERSON 1963] etc.

list of prime numbers between 2 and 100 is to be generated. A
first, very simple, not very scalable, straightforward solution
in C might look like this:

```
1   #include <stdio.h>
2
3   #define END 100
4
5   int is_prime(int value)
6   {
7       int divisor;
8
9       if (!(value % 2))
10          return value == 2;
11
12      for (divisor = 3; divisor * divisor <= value;
13           divisor += 2)
14          if (!(value % divisor))
15              return 0;
16
17      return 1;
18  }
19
20  int main()
21  {
22      int i;
23
24      for (i = 2; i <= END; i++)
25          if (is_prime(i))
26              printf("%d ", i);
27
28      printf("\n");
29      return 0;
30  }
```

A function is_prime() is defined which tests by successive division if a number is prime. Using this function within
a loop a list of prime numbers is printed. As simple as this approach is, a substantial amount of code is still not devoted to
the problem itself but is owed to the language used. Of course,
the function is_prime() is hopelessly slow as it performs the
same test divisions over and over again.

A more elegant and efficient solution in C could implement the *sieve of* ERATOSTHENES which is based on a unit stride vector starting with the value 2. It is obvious that at start the leftmost vector element must be prime, so all of its multiples can be marked as non-prime in a first run through the vector until the last vector element has been reached. The next loop will then determine the following element from the left which has not already been marked as being non-prime, removing all of its multiples etc. In the end the vector will contain a list of prime numbers. A typical C implementation of this algorithm might look as follows:

```
1    #include <stdio.h>
2    #include <stdlib.h>
3    #include <math.h>
4
5    int main()
6    {
7        int n, *a, i, j;
8
9        printf("Please enter maximum value: ");
10       scanf("%d", &n);
11
12       /* + 1 makes things more easy :-) */
13       if (!(a = malloc(sizeof (int) * (n + 1))))
14       {
15           perror("malloc() failed!");
16           return -1;
17       }
18
19       /* Mark every element as potentially prime */
20       for (i = 2; i <= n; a[i++] = 1);
21
22       for (i = 2; i <= (int) sqrt((double) n); i++)
23       {
24           /* Skip element if it is not prime */
25           if (a[i] != 1)
26               continue;
27
28           /* Get rid of i's multiples */
29           for (j = i << 1; j <= n; j += i)
30               a[j] = 0;
```

```
31        }
32
33        /* Print all prime numbers found */
34        for (i = 2; i <= n; i++)
35            if (a[i])
36                printf("%d ", i);
37
38        printf("\n");
39        return 0;
40  }
```

This solution is much more elegant than the simple trial divisions shown before, but the algorithm itself is rather cluttered by the properties and requirements of the language C itself. Solving this problem in an array language like APL might look like this instead:

$$(\sim E \in E \circ . \times E)/E \leftarrow 1 \downarrow \iota E \leftarrow 100$$

Isn't it fascinating? Dozens of lines of C-code have been replaced by a single – although arcane looking – line of APL-code.

How does this work? Reading the line from right to left, a scalar variable E is first set to the value 100. Applying the $\iota$ function to E yields a unit stride vector containing 100 elements: $(1, 2, \ldots, 100)$. Dropping the first element of this vector by $1 \downarrow$ in turn yields a vector $(2, 3, \ldots, 100)$ which is then stored again in the variable E.[10]

The next step is building a matrix by computing the outer product of two of these vectors: $E \circ . \times E$ applies the multiplication operator $\times$ to all combinations of elements from the two instances of E, effectively yielding a matrix of the form

$$\begin{pmatrix} 4 & 6 & 8 & 10 & \ldots \\ 6 & 9 & 12 & 15 & \ldots \\ 8 & 12 & 16 & 20 & \ldots \\ 10 & 15 & 20 & 25 & \ldots \\ \vdots & \vdots & \vdots & \vdots & \ddots \end{pmatrix}.$$

This particular matrix obviously does not contain prime numbers at all since every element of this matrix is the product of at least two prime numbers. By applying $E \in$ to this

---

[10]It should be noted that the variable E first held a scalar value and now contains a vector without any need for redefinition.

matrix, a binary vector is generated which corresponds to the vector E, containing a 1 at every place where E contains a non-prime number and a 0 otherwise. Inverting this vector by ~ yields a binary vector containing a 1 at every location corresponding to a prime number in E and a 0 everywhere else.

The last step is the selection of all elements from the original vector E based on this selection vector yielding a list of primes between 2 and 100.

The most remarkable thing about this program is the observation that no explicit loops and conditionals at all and only a minimal amount of variables are required. This is a characteristic feature of all array programming languages yielding terse and very expressive programs. Nevertheless, it should also be admitted that this program is not terribly efficient – but it is extremely elegant.

Of course, there is much more to write about array programming and APL in particular but these two examples might suffice as teasers by showing some of the power of the array programming paradigm. The following chapter now focuses on the basic design of Lang5.

# Chapter 2

# The design of Lang5

## 2.1 Reverse Polish notation

Most programming languages currently in use are based on an algebraic notation style which allows expressions like

```
z += dx * (y + 2 * (ya + yb) + yc) / 6
```

to be written. Typically, the evaluation of such expressions is performed in a left-to-right fashion and takes operator precedences into account. This seems useful and natural, but often unclear or erroneous assumptions about these operator precedences on the side of the programmer turn out to be the source of either unnecessary parentheses or of plain programming errors.

Accordingly, Ken Iverson decided to abandon this scheme for his APL system and employ a strict right-to-left scheme of evaluation with explicit parentheses as the primary means of ensuring operator precedence. This seems odd at first sight but it turns out that expressions written like this tend to be shorter and not as error-prone as those written in the traditional style as the following example shows: Evaluating a polynomial $(a, b, c, d, e) \prod x$ using the Horner scheme looks like

```
y = a + x * (b + x * (c + x * (d + x * e)))
```

when written as a traditional algebraic expression. Using Iverson's notation it is simplified to y = a + x * b + x * c + x * d + x * e.

The implementation of a parser for algebraic expressions
working in APL-style from right to left is shown in the following listing which is mainly based on [HOLUB 1985][pp. 165 ff.]:

```
1    /*
2    **   Simple parser for arithmetic integer
3    ** expressions of the following form:
4    **
5    **         <expression> = <factor>
6    **                      | <factor> [/+-*] <factor>
7    **
8    **         <factor>    = (<expression>)
9    **                     | -(<expression>)
10   **                     | <constant>
11   **                     | -<constant>
12   **
13   **         <constant>   = [0-9]
14   **                     | <constant>[0-9]
15   **
16   */
17
18   #include <stdio.h>
19   #include <string.h>
20   #include <ctype.h>
21
22   #define STRING_LENGTH 133
23
24   char *gbl_pos;      /* Pointer into the string to
25                          be parsed.  */
26   int gbl_error = 0; /* Error flag - incremented by
27                          each error. */
28
29   int expression();
30
31   /*
32   **   Get rid of an optional '\n' character at the
33   ** end of a string.
34   */
35   void chomp(char *string)
36   {
```

```
37      int last = strlen(string) - 1;
38      if (last >= 0 && string[last] == '\n')
39          string[last] = (char) 0;
40  }
41
42  /* Parse a constant and return its int value. */
43  int constant()
44  {
45      int result = 0;
46
47      /*
48      ** Loop over the digits of the constant
49      ** and update the result.
50      */
51      while (*gbl_pos && isdigit(*gbl_pos))
52          result = result * 10 + (*gbl_pos++ - '0');
53
54      return result;
55  }
56
57  /* Evaluate a factor in an expression. */
58  int factor()
59  {
60      int minus, result;
61
62      /*
63      ** Check for an optional minus sign,
64      ** remember, and get rid of it.
65      */
66      if ((minus = (*gbl_pos == '-')))
67          gbl_pos++;
68
69      /* Factor begins with a parenthesis */
70      if (*gbl_pos == '(')
71      {
72          gbl_pos++; /* Skip the parenthesis. */
73          result = expression();
74          if (gbl_error) return 0;
75
76          if (*gbl_pos == ')')
77              gbl_pos++;
78      }
```

```
 79        else
 80        /* No parenthesis, just a constant. */
 81            result = constant();
 82
 83        return minus ? -result : result;
 84    }
 85
 86    int expression() /* Evaluate an expression. */
 87    {
 88        char operator;
 89        int result, expr;
 90
 91        /*
 92        **  If an expression ends with an operator
 93        ** not followed by another factor we will
 94        ** end up here with gbl_pos pointing to the
 95        ** trailing null character of the string,
 96        ** which denotes an error.
 97        */
 98        if (!*gbl_pos)
 99        {
100            printf("\texpression(): Empty string!\n");
101            gbl_error++;
102            return 0;
103        }
104
105        /*
106        **  An expression consists of at least one
107        ** factor.
108        */
109        result = factor();
110        if (gbl_error) return 0;
111
112        /*
113        **  If there are chars left, the next one
114        ** must be an operator.
115        */
116        if (*gbl_pos)
117        {
118            operator = *gbl_pos++;
119
120            /* Calculate <expr> <operator> <expr>. */
```

```
121          switch(operator)
122          {
123              case '+':
124                  result += expression();
125                  break;
126              case '-':
127                  result -= expression();
128                  break;
129              case '*':
130                  result *= expression();
131                  break;
132              case '/':
133                  result /= expression();
134                  break;
135          }
136      }
137
138      return result;
139  }
140
141  int main()
142  {
143      char string[STRING_LENGTH];
144      int result;
145
146      /*
147      **  Endless loop for user input and
148      ** processing.
149      */
150      for(;;)
151      {
152          printf("Expression: ");
153
154          /*
155          **  Read user input - leave the
156          ** loop on EOFi.
157          */
158          if (!fgets(string, sizeof(string), stdin))
159              break;
160
161          chomp(string);
162
```

```
163          /*
164          **  All functions rely on this
165          ** global pointer.
166          */
167          gbl_pos = string;
168
169          result = expression();
170          if (gbl_error) /* Any errors so far? */
171          {
172              printf("\tError evaluating \"%s\"\n",
173                      string);
174              /* Reset error counter */
175              gbl_error = 0;
176          }
177          else
178              printf("\tResult = %d\n", result);
179      }
180
181      printf("Parser ended.\n");
182      return 0;
183  }
```

**Exercise 1:**

1. Extend the parser by adding binary operators for exponentiation (**), modulo (%) etc.

2. Add a unary operator ! to calculate the factorial of a
   number.

3. Change the parser so that it evaluates expressions
   from left to right.

Still another notation was developed by the Polish logician
and philosopher JAN ŁUKASIEWICZ.[1] He created what became
known as *Polish notation* or *prefix notation* in which an operator always precedes its operands. If the arity of all operators[2]
is fixed, this style of notation does not require any parentheses

---

[1] 12/21/1878–02/13/1956

[2] The arity describes how many operands an operator takes. In traditional
mathematical notation the minus-operator may be unary when used to change
the sign of a single variable like in $-x$ or may be binary as in $a - b$.

at all since the precedence of operations is solely determined by their position in an expression.[3] A variant of this notation, called *reverse Polish notation*, or *RPN* for short, was developed independently several times starting with [BURKS et al. 1954]. The programming language Forth, developed by CHARLES H. MOORE beginning in the late 1950s, is completely based on RPN as were most of HP's pocket calculators. Another example for an RPN language is PostScript which is used to describe and generate vector graphics.

RPN systems are based on a so-called *stack*, a data structure based on a list which can be extended by *pushing* elements onto it. Retrieving elements is done by an operation called *pop* which removes one element from the top of the stack and returns this element. Stacks are ubiquitous in modern computing as they are used to store parameters, local variables and return-addresses for subroutine or function calls. Therefore most modern processor architectures feature at least basic stack operations like push and pop. It is only in RPN programming languages like Forth or Lang5 that stacks are explicitly exposed to the programmer as central data structures.

Evaluating the polynomial shown above on an RPN system like a traditional HP pocket calculator could be done by the following sequence of operations, which looks a bit awkward at first sight but soon becomes second nature:

```
e x * d + x * c + x * b + x * a +.
```

This would, in effect, first push e and x onto the stack (i. e. their respective values), execute the binary multiplication operator *, which in turn removes the two topmost elements from the stack and pushes the result of the multiplication back onto the stack. This value is then incremented by d, multiplied by x and so on.

When designing a programming language, the first thing to determine is the way in which expressions should be written. Lang5 employs the RPN notation which has several advantages: It is rather easily implemented in an interpreter or compiler and programming in RPN-style turns out to be quite

---

[3]As JENS BREITENBACH points out, the Polish notation is more natural from a mathematical point of view than the common infix notation, since arithmetic operations are represented by functions taking two arguments: $p : \mathbb{N} \times \mathbb{N} \to \mathbb{N}, (x, y) \mapsto p(x, y) := x + y$.

powerful. In addition to that, it is especially useful in practice
to see the progression of a complex calculation. The following
code-example shows a simple RPN-calculator written in Perl:

```
 1  use strict;
 2  use warnings;
 3
 4  my @s;
 5
 6  my %functions = (
 7    '.' => sub {
 8                print pop(@s), "\n";
 9              },
10    '+' => sub {
11                push(@s, pop(@s) + pop(@s));
12              },
13    '*' => sub {
14                push(@s, pop(@s) * pop(@s));
15              },
16    '-' => sub {
17                push(@s, -(pop(@s) - pop(@s)));
18              },
19    '/' => sub {
20                push(@s, 1 / (pop(@s) / pop(@s)));
21              },
22  );
23
24  while (my $input = <STDIN>)
25  {
26    $functions{$_} ? $functions{$_}->() :
27                     push(@s, $_)
28      for (split(/\s+/, $input));
29    print "\tStack contents: ";
30    print "$_ " for @s;
31    print "\n";
32  }
```

At its heart is the stack which is just a global array.[4] The
basic functions offered are stored as subroutine references in
a hash %functions. The user input is read from the standard

---

[4]Being an introductory example, no provisions have been made for avoiding
a global stack or implementing error checking etc.

input channel and stored in the scalar variable $input. This line of input is then split on white-space characters to yield individual tokens which are then either used to execute a particular function or to push a value onto the stack.

If a token contains the name of a known operator or function, it is a valid key for the hash %functions. In these cases, the subroutine addressed by this key is executed,

    $functions{$_}->(),

in all other cases the token is pushed onto the stack. Using this simple program, an algebraic expression like 3 * 2 + 1 can be evaluated by entering 1 2 3 * + . – the single dot removes the topmost stack element and prints it to the standard output.

**Exercise 2:**

1. Extend this simple RPN calculator by adding binary operators for exponentiation (**), modulo (%) etc.

2. Extend it by adding a unary operator ! for calculating factorials.

3. Implement some basic error checking to make sure that there are enough elements on the stack for the various operations implemented. Ideally these checking routines would be implemented in a general way – one for all binary operators etc. One approach to accomplish this would be to change the hash %functions to a two-dimensional structure in which each function name points to a two-element hash containing two keys code and type. The value of code contains the reference to the actual routine performing the desired operation while type contains information about the routine as being of type unary, binary etc. This information could then be used to access a central error checking routine.

Of these three methods, left-to-right, and right-to-left evaluation of arithmetic expressions, and RPN, the latter one was selected as the basis for Lang5.

## 2.2   Dynamic typing

Another central aspect of programming languages is the question of whether to employ static typing as found for example in C or to use dynamic typing as used by most *dynamic programming languages*.[5] There is an ongoing discussion between proponents of these two paradigms. In static typing a variable gets a type like being an *integer* or a *float* assigned once and will be capable of holding a value of this type only during its life-time. This has several advantages – among others, it speeds up execution of programs since the type of a variable is known in advance and does not have to be determined during run-time. In addition to that, static typing allows a variety of programming errors to be caught during compile-time.

Dynamic typing, on the other hand, offers a high degree of flexibility: Why should one explicitly restrict a variable to holding only a single type of value while the executing instance, normally an interpreter, knows best which type a variable contains at run-time? The often expressed fear that this might open Pandora's box and yield errors hard to catch has not been proven over the years, instead, the application of languages using dynamic typing often yields significant productivity gains compared with languages based on a static typing concept[6] while not, as often feared, resulting in lower quality products.

It was decided to use dynamic typing in Lang5. In effect, most of Perl's dynamic typing capabilities are used in Lang5 since the interpreter is written entirely in Perl. So a scalar element on the stack can hold integer values, floating point numbers as well as strings.

## 2.3   Data structures

If it were just for the two characteristics of employing RPN in conjunction with dynamic typing, Lang5 would be nothing more than a slightly generalized Forth. But since Lang5 was intended to be an array language, the RPN concept was extended in a way that allows nested arrays to be pushed onto the stack and processed as a whole. So the two basic data

---

[5]Also known as *scripting languages* although this term lacks a precise definition and is not recommended.

[6]See [OUSTERHOUT 1998] and [PRECHELT 2010].

structures employed by Lang5 are scalar values like integers, floating point numbers and strings, and nested arrays of arbitrary dimension using scalars as their data elements. In this respect, Lang5 works quite like RPL, short for *Reverse Polish LISP*, the programming language used in late HP pocket calculators like the HP28 or HP48 and later models.

In Lang5 it is for example possible to push a nested data structure like the two-dimensional array

$$\begin{pmatrix} 1 & 2 & 3 \\ 4 & 5 & 6 \\ 7 & 8 & 9 \end{pmatrix}$$

onto the stack by entering

    [[1 2 3] [4 5 6] [7 8 9]]

This, of course, makes it necessary to extend the basic operators to work on $n$-dimensional data structures like this array as a whole instead of working on scalar values only. This is done implicitly by the interpreter which traverses data structures as necessary and applies basic operators like +, * etc. in an element-wise fashion to corresponding elements of such data structures.

The following chapter describes the process of installing and running the Lang5-interpreter which will be used throughout the remaining sections of this book. Afterwards, the language itself is introduced and described in detail.

## Chapter 3

# Installing and running Lang5

## 3.1 Installation

Since the Lang5-interpreter is written in pure Perl, it is highly
portable and can be installed easily on most operating systems.[1] The only prerequisite is, of course, a Perl interpreter.
If there is no Perl interpreter already installed on the destination system, this should be done first.[2]

The easiest way to get started with Lang5 is to download
the distribution kit lang5.zip from[3]

```
http://lang5.sourceforge.net
```

which can be unzipped to any suitable location in the directory structure of the destination system. There is no need to
install Lang5 into a special location like /usr/local or something like that on a UNIX system as the following example
shows.[4] Figure 3.1 shows the directory structure which will
be created by unzipping the Lang5-distribution kit as shown
in the following:

---

[1]Currently known installations run on LINUX, Mac OS X, Windows, and
OpenVMS (VAX, Alpha, and Itanium).

[2]Typical Perl distributions for most common operating systems can be ob-
tained from http://www.perl.org/get.html.

[3]The direct link is https://downloads.sourceforge.net/project/lang5/
lang5.zip.

[4]For a more permanent installation the PATH variable should be extended
accordingly to include the interpreter's base directory.

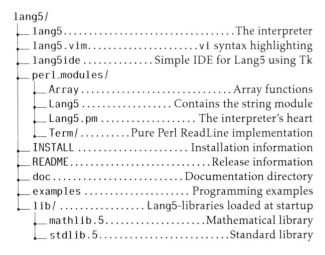

```
lang5/
├── lang5 ...............................The interpreter
├── lang5.vim.....................vi syntax highlighting
├── lang5ide .............Simple IDE for Lang5 using Tk
├── perl_modules/
│   ├── Array...........................Array functions
│   ├── Lang5 ................. Contains the string module
│   ├── Lang5.pm ................... The interpreter's heart
│   └── Term/.........Pure Perl ReadLine implementation
├── INSTALL ..................... Installation information
├── README...........................Release information
├── doc .......................... Documentation directory
├── examples .................... Programming examples
└── lib/ ................Lang5-libraries loaded at startup
    ├── mathlib.5...................Mathematical library
    └── stdlib.5........................Standard library
```

*Figure 3.1:* Directory structure created by the Lang5-distribution kit

```
1  $ cd
2  $ unzip ../Downloads/lang5.zip
3  Archive:  lang5.zip
4      ... ... ...
5  $ cd lang5
6  $ chmod 755 lang5
7  $ ~/lang5/lang5
8  loading mathlib.5: Const.. ...
9  loading stdlib.5:  Const..Misc..Stk..Struct..
10 lang5> exit
11 $
```

The installation on a Windows system is equally simple (provided that there is a Perl interpreter already installed): The distribution kit lang5.zip can be unzipped to any suitable location even something like C:\Temp\lang5. The interpreter is then started simply from within a command window[5] by typing the following command:

```
perl c:\Temp\lang5\lang5
```

---

[5]This can be opened by executing cmd.exe.

## 3.2  Starting the interpreter

In the simplest case the Lang5-interpreter is just started as shown above, but there are many cases which require the use of so-called "qualifiers" which control the overall behavior of the interpreter. The general format for calling the interpreter is as follows:

```
lang5 [<qualifier> [<qualifier>..[<qualifier>]..]]
     [file1 [file2 ...]]
```

file_1 etc. represent the names of files containing Lang5-source code that is to be executed by the interpreter. The available qualifiers are those listed below:[6]

-b or -benchmark: By specifying this qualifier, the interpreter will print a sorted list of call-frequencies for all functions, operators, and words which have been executed during a program run.

-d or -debug_level: This qualifier sets the debug level of the interpreter which is useful mainly during development of the interpreter itself. Possible values are TRACE, DEBUG, INFO, WARN, ERROR (this is the default value for this parameter), and FATAL. The latter value generates the least amount of output while TRACE generates *extremely* detailed output and should only be specified when it is necessary to debug the interpreter itself. Typing

```
lang5 -d TRACE
```

would start the interpreter in its trace mode where even the tiniest operation within the interpreter is logged.

-e or -evaluate: Using this qualifier it is possible to evaluate a Lang5-expression during startup of the interpreter and before loading any files containing Lang5-source code. This is useful to place initial values onto the stack or

---

[6]The prompt of the system where these commands were executed is alberich$. This prompt will occur in some of the examples in the following text – it does not have to be typed in!

to execute so-called *one-liners.*[7]  This option forces the
interpreter into batch mode:[8]

```
1  alberich$ lang5 -e "1 2 + ."
2  loading mathlib.5: Const.. ...
3  loading stdlib.5:  Const..Misc..Stk..Struct..
4  3
5  alberich$
```

-f **or** -format: By default, numerical values are printed by
   the Lang5-interpreter with at least four places to ensure
   a nicely formatted output of nested arrays. In cases where
   this default behavior is not suitable, the control string
   for all output operations can be modified by this parameter. To have output values printed with at least 15
   places, the interpreter could be started as follows:

```
1  alberich$ lang5 -format "%15s"
2  loading mathlib.5: Const.. ...
3  loading stdlib.5:  Const..Misc..Stk..Struct..
4  lang5> [1 2] .
5  [               1               2  ]
```

-i **or** -interactive: When the interpreter is started without
   any file name specified on the command line, it will automatically enter interactive mode. If one or more files
   containing Lang5-source code are specified, the interpreter will run in batch mode by default, so it will execute the code and then quit. In cases where files should
   be loaded and the interpreter should nevertheless run in
   interactive mode, this can be forced by specifying this
   qualifier on the command line.

-n **or** -nolibs: By default, the interpreter loads all libraries
   located in the lib directory of the interpreter's directory
   tree. Specifying this qualifier, loading these libraries can
   be suppressed:

---

[7]Small programs consisting only of one line of code are called one-liners.

[8]More than one -e-qualifier may be supplied at once. If there are any source
code files specified on the command line, they will be executed after the statements following -e have been executed.

```
1   alberich$ lang5
2   loading mathlib.5: Const.. ...
3   loading stdlib.5:  Const..Misc..Stk..Struct..
4   lang5> exit
5
6   alberich$ lang5 -n
7   lang5> exit
8   alberich$
```

-sta or -statistics: The -statistics qualifier behaves like
    -benchmark with the difference that the output will not
    be sorted by the number of calls made to the various
    functions, operators and words.

-ste or -steps: This parameter expects an integer argument
    which limits the interpreter to executing only a limited
    number of instructions. In addition to this, the use of
    -steps automatically disables the execution of system
    calls. This behaviour was implemented to allow Lang5
    to be used in a CGI webserver environment.

-t or -time: Specifying -t, the interpreter will print out the
    time consumed for each line executed when running in
    interactive mode. When running in batch mode, the to-
    tal run time will be printed.

-v or -version: This qualifier causes the interpreter to print
    out its version number before executing any program.[9]

-w or -width: Some commands are aware of the current ter-
    minal width which is set to 80 by default. Using -w this
    width can be changed.

## 3.3   First steps

With a Lang5-interpreter installed it is time for some hands-on
experience. The very first example to be given is the archetypical hello-world-program written in Lang5. The first example shows how to write and run a hello-world in interactive
mode:

---

[9]The libraries are loaded before printing the version number.

```
1   alberich$ lang5
2   loading mathlib.5: Const.. ...
3   loading stdlib.5:  Const..Misc..Stk..Struct..
4   lang5> "Hello world!\n" .
5   Hello world!
6   lang5> exit
```

Now create a file called hello_world.5 with your preferred text-editor.[10] This file should consist of only one line containing the program typed in in the above example. This program is then executed by running the Lang5-interpreter in batch mode which is entered automatically if a file name is specified when starting the interpreter:

```
1   alberich$ cat > hello_word.5
2   "Hello world!\n" .
3   alberich$ lang5 hello_word.5
4   loading mathlib.5: Const.. ...
5   loading stdlib.5:  Const..Misc..Stk..Struct..
6   loading hello_word.5
7   Hello world!
8   alberich$
```

Now let us execute some of the examples supplied with the Lang5-interpreter:

```
1    alberich$ lang5 -b lang5/examples/sine_curve.5
2    loading mathlib.5: Const.. ...
3    loading stdlib.5:  Const..Misc..Stk..Struct..
4    loading lang5/examples/sine_curve.5
5                               *
6                                   *
7                                      *
8                                        *
9                                          *
10                                          *
11                                         *
12                                       *
13                                   *
```

---

[10]The UNIX shell command cat used in the following is far from being an editor but is useful in short examples like this.

```
14                                           *
15                                      *
16                          *
17                     *
18                *
19             *
20             *
21             *
22                *
23                   *
24                        *
25                              *
26   =================================================
27   Statistics:
28   -------------------------------------------------
29   execute word      :  572 ! Function           :  438 !
30   Push data         :  275 ! Binary             :  130 !
31   +                 :   64 ! If                 :   63 !
32   compress          :   63 ! Word definitions   :   61 !
33   Max. stack depth  :   50 ! roll               :   42 !
34   swap              :   42 ! _roll              :   42 !
35   dup               :   42 ! expand             :   42 !
36   type              :   42 ! .                  :   39 !
37   ne                :   21 ! append             :   21 !
38   eq                :   21 ! <                  :   21 !
39   depth             :   21 ! join               :   21 !
40   reshape           :   21 ! Unary              :    4 !
41   *                 :    2 ! /                  :    1 !
42   int               :    1 ! iota               :    1 !
43   print_dot         :    1 ! sin                :    1 !
44   -------------------------------------------------
45   alberich$
```

# Chapter 4

# Lang5 basics

As already described, Lang5 is a small interpreted programming language borrowing heavily from APL and Forth. Lang5
attempts to combine the particular strengths of Forth (basically its stack based structure and the ability to extend the
language itself by defining so-called *words* which can then be
used in exactly the same way as built-in functions or operators) with those of APL (especially its array handling capabilities).

## 4.1   Getting started

As already mentioned, Lang5 is built around a stack as its central data structure. Such a stack is a list which basically allows
access only to elements on its end thus forming a *LIFO*[1] data
structure.  Elements are said to be *pushed* to and *popped* or
sometimes *pulled* from the stack.

Using a stack oriented language like Charles H. Moore's
Forth or in this case Lang5, typically feels a bit awkward for
the uninitiated, so don't be frightened away by the following
sections.

As an example, the expression (2+3)*4 is to be evaluated
with Lang5. One way to do this is to push all arguments onto
the stack and the applying the necessary binary operators +
and *:

---

[1] Short for *Last In First Out*.

```
lang5> 4 3 2 + * .
20
```

The interpreter will push anything to its stack as long as it is not an operator or any other objects[2] that can be executed. Individual values, function names, operators etc. are delimited by white space like a blank character or a newline, so 4 3 2 pushes three scalar values onto the stack which will then contain the value 2 in its topmost position afterwards. This topmost position of a stack is called *Top Of Stack*, *TOS* for short.

Executing a binary operator will always fetch the two topmost elements from the stack (if there are not enough elements on the stack, an error is thrown), use them as operands for the operator and push the result back onto the stack. So executing the binary operator + in the above example will pop the two topmost elements of the stack (2 and 3), add them and push the resulting value 5 back onto the stack which now contains the values 4 and 5.

Executing the binary operator * will then remove these two values from the stack and push back the result of the multiplication which is 20 in this case. The function . finally removes the topmost element from the stack and prints it, leaving the stack empty.

> **Exercise 3:**
> 1. Calculate the area of a circle with a diameter of 1.25 meters using the Lang5-interpreter. (Hint: pi pushes an approximation for $\pi$ onto the stack.)
>
> 2. Devise as many different ways as you can imagine to compute the sum of the values 2, 3, 5, 8, and 13 using Lang5.

It should be noted that everything in a line following the #-character will be ignored by the interpreter and treated as a comment.[3] As important as comments are in more traditional languages, they are even more important in an extremely concise language like Lang5. It is not uncommon to have more comments than actual statements in a typical Lang5-program.

---

[2]Not in the sense of *object* in object oriented programming languages.

[3]As of now, Lang5 currently does not support multiline comments.

## 4.2 Basic data structures

So the central data structure within Lang5 is a stack. In contrast to Forth this stack can hold not only scalar values as shown in the preceding section but arrays of arbitrary structure.[4] Thus Lang5 distinguishes between scalar values and arrays which are pushed onto the stack. Examples for scalar values are 3.1415926535, 17654 or even a string like "Hello world!":[5]

```
1   lang5> 3.1415926535
2
3   lang5> 17
4
5   lang5> "Hello world!"
6
7   lang5> .s
8   vvvvvvvvvv Begin of stack listing vvvvvvvvvv
9   Stack contents (TOS at bottom):
10  3.1415926535
11  17
12  Hello world!
13  ^^^^^^^^^^^ End of stack listing ^^^^^^^^^^^
```

So far so good, but the real power of Lang5 stems from its ability to deal with arbitrarily deeply nested arrays on the stack. An array is denoted be enclosing its values into square brackets as the following examples of a one-, a two- and a three-dimensional array show:

```
1   lang5> [1]
2
3   lang5> [[1 2][3 4]]
4
5   lang5> [[[1 2][3 4]][[5 6][7 8]]]
6
7   lang5> .s
8   vvvvvvvvvv Begin of stack listing vvvvvvvvvv
9   Stack contents (TOS at bottom):
```

---

[4]The term *array* will always denote an array of arbitrary dimension in the following.

[5]Using .s the current contents of the stack can be displayed without destroying the stack's contents as a repetitive application of . would do.

```
10   [       1    ]
11   [
12     [       1        2    ]
13     [       3        4    ]
14   ]
15   [
16     [
17       [       1        2    ]
18       [       3        4    ]
19     ]
20     [
21       [       5        6    ]
22       [       7        8    ]
23     ]
24   ]
25   ^^^^^^^^^^^ End of stack listing ^^^^^^^^^^^
```

Sometimes it is necessary to push an operator onto the stack rather than executing it directly. In this case it can be enclosed either in double quotes to force the interpreter to accept it as a simple string or it can be preceded with a single quote like this:[6]

```
1   lang5> "+" .
2   +
3   lang5> '- .
4   -
```

Many operators and functions built into Lang5 work on scalars as well as on arrays. If a unary function like the factorial ! is applied to a scalar it just returns the corresponding factorial. If its argument is an array it will be automatically applied to all array elements:

```
1   lang5> 5 ! .
2   120
3   lang5> [0 1 2 3 4 5] ! .
4   [    1      1      2      6      24      120    ]
```

---

[6]This also pushes a string onto the stack as long as the string itself does not contain any whitespace characters.

The same mechanism applies to binary operators and functions, so arrays can be easily added, multiplied, divided, subtracted etc. in an element-wise fashion:

```
1  lang5> [1 2] [3 4] + .
2  [    4    6  ]
```

What happens if the data structures are not "compatible" with respect to their *shape*? The Lang5-interpreter first determines which of the two structures supplied as operands to a binary operator or function is bigger and then transforms the shape of the smaller to match that of the bigger structure. Since the smaller array does not contain enough elements for this transformation, its elements are used over and over again to fill the required intermediate data structure. This also applies to extreme cases where a binary operator or function is applied to an array and a scalar:

```
1  lang5> [1 2 3] [4 5] + .
2  [    5    7    7  ]
3  lang5> [1 2 3] 1 + .
4  [    2    3    4  ]
```

> **Exercise 4:**
> 1. Compute and print the sum of the two following two-dimensional matrices:
>
> $$\begin{pmatrix} 1 & 2 & 3 \\ 4 & 5 & 6 \\ 7 & 8 & 9 \end{pmatrix} \text{ and } \begin{pmatrix} 7 & 6 & 2 \\ 1 & 9 & 5 \\ 3 & 8 & 4 \end{pmatrix}.$$
>
> 2. Subtract the value 1 from all elements of the first matrix shown above and print the result.

## 4.3 Language elements

The basic language elements of Lang5 are divided into built-in operators, functions, control instructions and so-called *words* which are user-defined and can be used exactly like built-ins after their definition. This makes it possible to extend the language itself by defining words which are then used in programs. The following terms are used in the remaining portion of this book:

### 4.3.1   Operators

Since Lang5 is a stack based language as Forth, everything has to be written in post-fix notation with

- *niladic*,
- *unary*, and
- *binary*

operators. These will fetch 0, 1 or 2 elements from the stack, perform some operation on these values and push the result back onto the stack. Examples for operators are the well known basic arithmetic operators like +, -, both being binary, and the like.

As shown in the previous examples, operators work on scalars only – if applied to arrays the Lang5-interpreter will traverse the nested data structure and apply the operator to the underlying scalar elements forming the actual array, so `[1 2 3] 1 +` will add one to every element of the array [1 2 3] yielding [2 3 4]. This holds true for unary as well as binary operators. If a binary operator is applied to two arrays these should be of the same shape and size – otherwise the dimensionally larger operand determines how the smaller operand will be restructured automatically prior to executing the operator – and the operator will then be applied to corresponding elements from each of the arrays.

In addition to that, binary operators (and binary user-defined words, see section 4.3.5) can be used in conjunction with the array operation outer which creates outer products and the like (see below) as well as with reduce which applies an operator or word to elements of an array yielding a result with a dimension which is lower by one than the dimension of the input array (more about that later).

Another noteworthy characteristic of operators is that they can have neutral elements. This is returned as result if the operator is applied an empty or undefined data structure or an undefined scalar.

### 4.3.2   Functions

While an operator works on scalars only and always pushes exactly one result value back onto the stack, so-called *functions* act in a more general way as they can operate on a value

on the stack as a whole and not in an element-wise fashion.
An example for such a function is dup which duplicates the
topmost stack element regardless of its structure:

```
lang5> [1 2 3] dup .s
vvvvvvvvvv Begin of stack listing vvvvvvvvvv
Stack contents (TOS at bottom):
[   1     2     3   ]
[   1     2     3   ]
^^^^^^^^^^ End of stack listing ^^^^^^^^^^
```

### 4.3.3   Control instructions

Lang5 features only a few so-called *control instructions* which
are used to implement conditional execution of program parts
and loops.[7] The most basic control instruction is the if-else-
then construction:[8]

```
lang5> 1 2 > if "greater" else "less/equal" then .
less or equal
```

The keyword if removes the topmost stack element and performs all actions up to the next else or then, whichever comes
first, if this value evaluates to something considered true. Typically, everything which is not 0 or undefined (undef) is considered as being false.

The only built-in loop construction is do-loop which implements an endless loop which can be terminated with break:

```
lang5> 1 do dup . 1 + dup 5 > if break then loop
1
2
3
4
5
```

**Exercise 5:**

Modify the program shown above so that the loop counts
down from 5 to 1 and then exits.

---

[7]See section 5.5 for a more detailed list of control instructions and their application.

[8]The else-part is optional.

### 4.3.4 I/O instructions

An I/O instruction[9] either reads or writes data from or to a
device (normally stdin and stdout if no I/O-redirection has
been executed). One of the output instructions, ., has been
used extensively in the preceding sections already, see section
5.3 for more information.

### 4.3.5 Words

A word is a user-defined collection of operators, functions,
constants etc. which can be accessed later on by issuing the
name of the word. Thus a word acts very much like a subroutine in a conventional programming language. User-defined
words come in three flavors:

**Simple words:** Basically, such a word acts like a function described above. It "sees" the stack as a whole and is free
to do whatever it wants with the stack contents.

**Unary words:** A unary word can be used exactly like a built
in unary operator. This also implies that it only "sees"
the topmost stack element on which it can operate.

**Binary words:** A binary word can be used like a binary operator (especially in conjunction with reduce and outer
etc.). Like a unary word, it is restricted to operate on the
two topmost stack elements.

The concept of user-defined words which has been pio-
neered in Forth is one of the main features of Lang5. Defining a simple word looks quite the same as it would in Forth:
The word definition itself is started with a colon, followed by a
white space and the name of the new word (or that of a word to
be overridden). All following commands are grouped into this
word until a white space separated semicolon is encountered
which terminates the word definition process. In the following example a word named square is defined which computes
the square of the topmost stack element:

---

[9]Short for *input/output* instruction.

```
1   lang5> : square dup * ;
2
3   lang5> 5 square .
4   25
```

Such a *simple* word works on the stack as a whole. It will not be applied in an element-wise fashion as will be binary operators or words, although in some cases it may look like this.

> **Exercise 6:**
>
> The square word defined above is applied to the topmost stack element as a whole – explain the behavior of the interpreter in this example:
>
> ```
> lang5> : square dup * ;
>
> lang5> [1 2 3] square .
> [    1    4    9  ]
> ```
>
> Why is the result a three-element vector as the original operand and why have the elements of the operand been squared if the word itself has *not* been applied implicitly to each vector element?

Things get more interesting when unary or binary words are defined since these behave exactly like other built-in unary and binary operators. In the following first example a unary word called print will be defined which will be applied automatically in an element-wise fashion by the Lang5-interpreter if its argument is not a scalar but an array:

```
1    lang5> : print(*) . ;
2
3    lang5> 1 print
4    1
5    lang5> [1 2 3] print
6    1
7    2
8    3
9    lang5> [[1 2][3 4]] print
10   1
```

```
11   2
12   3
13   4
```

The suffix (*) following the word's name makes it a unary
word. The star denotes that the interpreter does not have to
care about so-called *dressed data structures* which are described
later in section 4.4, so the word will be implicitly and automatically applied on every element of the data structure found on
the top of the stack by the interpreter itself.

A binary word is defined in the most simple case by specifying (**) as suffix of the word's name as the following example shows:[10]

```
1   lang5> : binary_print(*,*) . . "------\n" . ;
2
3   lang5> [1 2 3] [4 5 6] binary_print
4   4
5   1
6   ------
7   5
8   2
9   ------
10  6
11  3
12  ------
```

**Exercise 7:**

What will happen if this binary word binary_print is applied to a vector [1 2 3] and a scalar 1 instead of two vectors? Explain the behavior of the interpreter.

### 4.3.6   Variables

Although variables are required less often in Lang5 than in
most other programming languages, their use often makes a
program more readable and maintainable. Variables are set
using set which expects the name of the variable to be set on
the topmost stack element and the value which is to be stored
in the variable in the stack element just below. If the variable

---

[10]The control sequence \n used within a string generates a newline character
sequence.

did not exist before being set it will be created, otherwise its current value will be overwritten.

The value stored in a variable is pushed onto the stack by just entering the name of the variable:

```
lang5> 2 'x set

lang5> x x * .
4
```

Using the word .v a list of all variables currently defined can be displayed.[11]

> **Exercise 8:**
>
> Apply the simple word square defined above to a variable called vector which has been set to [1 2 3 4] before and print the result.

## 4.4 Dressed data structures

So-called *dressed data structures* are the basis for overloading words. As powerful as unary and binary user-defined words are, it is often necessary to make clear to what type of data such a word is to be applied by the interpreter. Therefore data structures on the stack can be marked by *dressing* them. This operation assigns a meta-information to a data structure without altering its contents.

A data structure can be dressed in two ways: either implicitly by writing the *dress code* enclosed in parentheses following the structure to be dressed or by explicitly using the dress function. In the following example two data structures are defined with the dress codes foo and bar:

```
lang5> [1 2](foo)

lang5> [3 4] 'bar dress

lang5> .s
vvvvvvvvvv Begin of stack listing vvvvvvvvvv
```

---

[11]This list also contains some special purpose variables which control the operation of the Lang5-interpreter – see appendix A – so it will not be empty upon startup of the interpreter.

```
 7   Stack contents (TOS at bottom):
 8   [    1     2   ](foo)
 9   [    3     4   ](bar)
10   ^^^^^^^^^^^ End of stack listing ^^^^^^^^^^^
```

Applying a simple unary word like print as defined above on these data structures will now fail since the interpreter will only apply it in an element-wise fashion to the elements of an undressed array! In the case of a dressed data structure the interpreter will search for a unary or binary word with the proper dress code which fails in this example:

```
 1   lang5> print
 2   Error: no handler for type 'bar'
```

Using the dress code it is now possible to overload the word print to deal with data structures having the dress code foo by simply following the word definition with the required dress code enclosed in parentheses:

```
 1   lang5> [1 2](foo)
 2
 3   lang5> : print(foo) "foo:" . .  ;
 4   lang5> print
 5   foo:[    1     2   ](foo)
 6   lang5> .s
 7   vvvvvvvvvv Begin of stack listing vvvvvvvvvv
 8   Stack contents (TOS at bottom):
 9   ^^^^^^^^^^^ End of stack listing ^^^^^^^^^^^
```

Why is there an undefined value on top of the stack now? The reason is simple: The unary word print with dress code (foo) has been applied to the data structure as a whole. Whatever this word returns on the stack will be used as the result of this word. Since the last . consumes the dressed data structure by printing it, there is no return value from print(foo) and thus the stack contains an undefined element instead of the original dressed data structure.

This brings up the following question: What does the word print(foo) "see" on the stack when it is being executed?

```
lang5> 1

lang5> [2 3](foo)

lang5> : print(foo) .s ;

lang5> .s
vvvvvvvvvv Begin of stack listing vvvvvvvvvv
Stack contents (TOS at bottom):
1
[    2    3  ](foo)
^^^^^^^^^^ End of stack listing ^^^^^^^^^^
lang5> print
vvvvvvvvvv Begin of stack listing vvvvvvvvvv
Stack contents (TOS at bottom):
[    2    3  ](foo)
^^^^^^^^^^ End of stack listing ^^^^^^^^^^
lang5> .s
vvvvvvvvvv Begin of stack listing vvvvvvvvvv
Stack contents (TOS at bottom):
1
[    2    3  ](foo)
^^^^^^^^^^ End of stack listing ^^^^^^^^^^
```

This needs some explanation: At first, two values, 1 and [2 3](foo), are pushed onto the stack as shown by the first .s. Another .s invoked as part of the definition of print(foo) only shows the dressed structure [2 3](foo) while a third .s invoked after the execution of print(foo) has completed shows both values again.

The reason for this is simple: All unary and binary words operate in a *stack jail*, i.e. they get a temporary stack which only contains the one (in the unary case) or two topmost elements (for binary words) read from the main stack. This makes it impossible for a word to have side effects on the main stack, since every such word gets its own temporary stack to work with, which is destroyed after completion of the word's execution. At this point the topmost element of this temporary stack is copied back to the main stack where it serves as the result of the word.

As complicated as dressed data structures may seem, they are very powerful and used in many places in the libraries of Lang5. Typical examples are the basic arithmetic operators which are overloaded in the mathematical library to work transparently on complex numbers. By convention, a complex number, consisting of a real and an imaginary part, is denoted by the dress code (c) like this:

```
1  lang5> [1 2](c) [3 4](c) * .
2  [    -5    10   ](c)
```

In contrast to this, two undressed arrays holding two scalar values each would just be multiplied in an element-wise fashion as the following example shows:

```
1  lang5> [1 2] [3 4] * .
2  [    3     8   ]
```

The definition of the overloaded multiplication word for complex numbers, which can be found in the mathematical library,[12] looks like this:[13]

```
1  # Multiplication of two complex numbers.
2  : *(c,c)
3    strip swap strip swap
4    [0 1 0 1] subscript swap [0 1 1 0] subscript
5    * expand drop
6    + rot rot - swap
7    2 compress 'c dress
8  ;
```

An essential operation employed by most of the words operating on dressed data structures can be seen at the beginning of this overloaded multiplication: Using the strip function, the data structures the word operates on are explicitly undressed – otherwise an endless recursion would occur if another multiplication became necessary in this word which would call the word again etc. swap is a typical function in stack oriented programming languages. It exchanges the two topmost stack elements, so in effect strip swap strip swap

---

[12]See section C.

[13]This serves just as an example since most of the functionality used here has not yet been introduced.

strips both operands making sure that their order on the temporary stack remains unchanged afterwards

**Exercise 9:**

Define an overloaded definition of the binary word *
which operates on two data structures dressed with (baz).
This new word shall multiply the elements of the two
operand vectors element-wise but with a change of sign.
The result should be a (baz) data structure again.

Currently, the five following dress codes are used in the
Lang5-libraries although additional dress codes can be introduced any time:

**c:** Complex numbers

**m:** Matrices

**p:** Polar coordinate tuples

**s:** Sets

**v:** Vectors

# Chapter 5

# The Lang5 dictionary

Lang5 comes with a decent complement of built-in functions, operators and words. These words are defined in so-called *libraries* which are loaded during startup and are contained in the lib directory of the Lang5-directory tree. The following sections describe all of these elements in alphabetical order in detail grouped as follows:

- Stack manipulation and display

- Array manipulation and generation

- File handling

- Mathematical, logical and comparison operations

- Control structures

- Miscellaneous operators and functions

- Variable and word handling

## 5.1 Stack manipulation and display

The following functions and words build the backbone of the stack manipulation capabilities of Lang5. They operate directly on the stack and do not care about the structure of any element on the stack, so swap will just interchange the two topmost stack elements regardless of their dress code or structure etc.

### 5.1.1 ..

This function is normally used for debugging purposes only since it prints the stack's contents using Perl's standard module Data::Dumper not yielding nicely formatted output. .. does not affect the values on the stack:

```
 1  lang5> 1 2 [3 4] [5 6](foo) ..
 2  $1 = [
 3     1,
 4     2,
 5     1,
 6     2,
 7     [
 8       '3',
 9       '4'
10     ],
11     1,
12     2,
13     [
14       '3',
15       '4'
16     ],
17     bless( [
18       '5',
19       '6'
20     ], 'foo' )
21  ];
```

### 5.1.2 .s

This word from the standard library[1] prints all elements on the stack in a non-destructive way using the standard output format of Lang5 which is pretty useful during program development:

```
 1  lang5> 1 2 [3 4] [5 6](foo) .s
 2  vvvvvvvvvv Begin of stack listing vvvvvvvvvv
 3  Stack contents (TOS at bottom):
 4  1
 5  2
```

---

[1] See section B.

```
 6  1
 7  2
 8  [    3     4    ]
 9  1
10  2
11  [    3     4    ]
12  [    5     6    ](foo)
13  1
14  2
15  [    3     4    ]
16  [    5     6    ](foo)
17  ^^^^^^^^^^ End of stack listing ^^^^^^^^^^
```

### 5.1.3   clear

This word from the standard library removes all elements from the stack:

```
1  lang5> 1 2 [3 4] [5 6](foo) clear .s
2  Stack is empty!
```

### 5.1.4   depth

The depth function pushes the number of elements stored in the stack onto the stack:

```
1  lang5> clear 1 2 [3 4] [5 6](foo) depth .
2  4
```

### 5.1.5   drop

This function removes the topmost element of the stack. An empty stack will cause an error:

```
1  lang5> clear 1 drop
2
3  lang5> drop
4  Error: too few elements on stack, expected X
5  History: drop clear depth 0 > if ARRAY(0x...) 1
6    drop drop
```

### 5.1.6 dup

The dup function duplicates the topmost stack element which is often useful for the conditional execution of program parts and the like:

```
1  lang5> clear [1 2] dup .s
2  vvvvvvvvvv Begin of stack listing vvvvvvvvvv
3  Stack contents (TOS at bottom):
4  [    1    2  ]
5  [    1    2  ]
6  ^^^^^^^^^^ End of stack listing ^^^^^^^^^^
```

### 5.1.7 2dup

This word from the standard library duplicates the two top-most stack elements:

```
1  lang5> clear 1 2 2dup .s
2  vvvvvvvvvv Begin of stack listing vvvvvvvvvv
3  Stack contents (TOS at bottom):
4  1
5  2
6  1
7  2
8  ^^^^^^^^^^ End of stack listing ^^^^^^^^^^
```

### 5.1.8 ndrop

ndrop, which is also defined in the standard library, drops the *n* topmost stack elements (not including the value *n* which is contained in the topmost stack element):

```
1  lang5> clear 1 2 3 2 ndrop .s
2  vvvvvvvvvv Begin of stack listing vvvvvvvvvv
3  Stack contents (TOS at bottom):
4  1
5  ^^^^^^^^^^ End of stack listing ^^^^^^^^^^
```

### 5.1.9 over

This function copies the second element from the top of stack to the top of stack:

```
1   lang5> clear 1 2 over .s
2   vvvvvvvvvv Begin of stack listing vvvvvvvvvv
3   Stack contents (TOS at bottom):
4   1
5   2
6   1
7   ^^^^^^^^^^ End of stack listing ^^^^^^^^^^
```

**Exercise 10:**

Define a new word twodup that works like 2dup using the over function.

### 5.1.10 pick

A generalized form of over is the word pick from the standard library. Controlled by a natural number on top of the stack it will pick the element *n* positions down the stack nondestructively and push a copy of this element on the stack:

```
1   lang5> clear 1 2 3 4 3 pick .s
2   vvvvvvvvvv Begin of stack listing vvvvvvvvvv
3   Stack contents (TOS at bottom):
4   1
5   2
6   3
7   4
8   1
9   ^^^^^^^^^^ End of stack listing ^^^^^^^^^^
```

**Exercise 11:**

Define yet another word performing the same action as 2dup, this time using pick.

### 5.1.11 _roll

This function implements a very generalized rotation on the elements on the stack. It expects the number of rotation steps in the topmost stack element and the depth the rotation shall cover in the element below:

```
1   lang5> clear 1 2 3 4 5 6 4 2 _roll .s
2   vvvvvvvvvv Begin of stack listing vvvvvvvvvv
```

```
3   Stack contents (TOS at bottom):
4   1
5   2
6   5
7   6
8   3
9   4
10  ^^^^^^^^^^^ End of stack listing ^^^^^^^^^^^
```

### 5.1.12  roll

This standard library word is a variant of _roll. It requires only the depth of the rotation to be performed in the topmost stack element. Each execution of roll will then perform a single rotation step.

> **Exercise 12:**
>
> Define a word called myroll based on _roll that behaves like roll.

### 5.1.13  rot

This word, defined in the standard library, is the equivalent to the classic Forth function and performs a single rotation on the three topmost stack elements:

```
1   lang5> clear 1 2 3 rot .s
2   vvvvvvvvvv Begin of stack listing vvvvvvvvvv
3   Stack contents (TOS at bottom):
4   2
5   3
6   1
7   ^^^^^^^^^^^ End of stack listing ^^^^^^^^^^^
```

### 5.1.14  swap

The swap function interchanges the two topmost stack elements:

```
1   lang5> 1 2 swap . .
2   1
3   2
```

> **Exercise 13:**
> Define a word myswap that implements the functionality
> of swap using only operations like rot, over and the like.

## 5.2 Array manipulation and generation

The functions, operators and words described in the following
implement the array capabilities of Lang5. In contrast to the
stack operations described above they are "aware" of the data
structures they act upon.

### 5.2.1 append

The append word defined in the standard library expects two
arrays or an array and a scalar in the two topmost stack elements and returns a larger array containing the concatenation
of the elements of these two operands:

```
lang5> [1 2] [3 4] append .
[    1     2     3     4  ]
lang5> [1 2] 3 append .
[    1     2     3  ]
```

### 5.2.2 apply

The function apply applies a unary or binary operator or user-
defined word along the first axis of an array (or two arrays) as
the following example shows:

```
lang5> [[1 2][3 4]]

lang5> : print(*) . ;

lang5> dup print
1
2
3
4
lang5> 'print apply
[    1     2  ]
[    3     4  ]
```

In the first example, the unary word print is executed
on a copy of the two-dimensional array [[1 2][3 4]]. Since
this word has been defined as a unary word denoted by the
suffix (*), the interpreter implicitly applies the word to every single element of the array, calling it four times. Using
apply this unary word is only called twice – once for each
one-dimensional sub-array of the original array yielding the
output shown at the bottom of the example.

### 5.2.3   collapse

The collapse function "flattens" a nested array and returns
a one-dimensional array containing all elements of the argument:

```
1   lang5> [[1 2][3 4]] collapse .
2   [    1    2    3    4  ]
```

### 5.2.4   compress

This function takes *n* elements from the stack and forms an
array from these elements. It expects the number of elements
to be fetched in the topmost stack element:

```
1   lang5> 1 2 3 4 4 compress .
2   [    1    2    3    4  ]
```

### 5.2.5   dreduce

This word from the standard library applies the reduce function (see section 5.2.17) repeatedly on a nested array structure
until only a scalar value is left. It expects a binary operator on
the topmost stack element and an array below. It then applies
this operator between each two successive array elements:

```
1   lang5> [[1 2][3 4]] '+ dreduce .
2   10
```

**Exercise 14:**

Implement a word mydreduce that performs the same operation as dreduce, based on reduce.

### 5.2.6   dress

The dress function *dresses* an array with a name, a so-called *dress code.*[2] The explicit form looks like `[1 2] 'c dress` while the same effect can be achieved with implicit dressing as in `[1 2](c)`.

### 5.2.7   dressed

This function returns the dress code of a dressed data structure – if applied to a non-dressed structure or a scalar yields an undefined valued:

```
lang5> [1 2](c) dressed .
c
lang5> 1 dressed .
undef
```

It should be noted that dressed does not remove the structure its operates on from the stack, it just pushes the dress code as a string onto the stack.

### 5.2.8   expand

expand is a function that expects an array in the topmost stack element. It removes this element from the stack and places all array elements along the first axis back onto the stack. After expanding the array in this way, the number of elements written to the stack is pushed onto the stack so that a following compress would recreate the original data structure:

```
lang5> clear [[1 2] [3 4] 5] expand .s
vvvvvvvvvv Begin of stack listing vvvvvvvvvv
Stack contents (TOS at bottom):
[    1     2  ]
[    3     4  ]
5
3
^^^^^^^^^^ End of stack listing ^^^^^^^^^^
```

---

[2]See section 4.4.

### 5.2.9  extract

This word from the standard library extracts a particular element from an array removing it from the array and placing the element just removed onto the stack:

```
lang5> clear ['this 'is 'a 'test] 2 extract .s
vvvvvvvvvv Begin of stack listing vvvvvvvvvv
Stack contents (TOS at bottom):
[ this is test ]
a
^^^^^^^^^^ End of stack listing ^^^^^^^^^^
```

### 5.2.10  grade

The grade function expects a one-dimensional array (a vector) in the topmost stack element and generates a vector of the same size containing index values which will yield a sorted vector if used as argument for a subscript function (see section 5.2.29):

```
lang5> clear [3 1 4 1 5 9 2 6 5 3 5] grade .s
vvvvvvvvvv Begin of stack listing vvvvvvvvvv
Stack contents (TOS at bottom):
[   3    1    4    1    5    9    2    6    5    3    5  ]
[   3    1    6    9    0    2    8    4   10    7    5  ]

^^^^^^^^^^ End of stack listing ^^^^^^^^^^
lang5> subscript .
[   1    1    2    3    3    4    5    5    5    6    9  ]
```

### 5.2.11  in

in implements the element-of function from set theory. It is best demonstrated with a simple example:

```
lang5> [1 3 5] [1 2 3 4 5] in .
[   1    0    1    0    1  ]
```

Using the select function (see section 5.2.23) the vector resulting from executing in can be used to select only those elements of a data structure having a non-zero value in corresponding locations of this result vector.

### 5.2.12   index

This function generates an index vector representing the first location of each of the elements of the structure found on the topmost stack element in the structure just below it. If an element is not contained in this structure an empty index element is returned:

```
lang5> [3 1 4 1 5 9 2 6 5 3 5] [1 2 3 4 5 6 7]
lang5> index .
[
    [     1  ]
    [     6  ]
    [     0  ]
    [     2  ]
    [     4  ]
    [     7  ]
    [ ]
]
```

### 5.2.13   iota

This unary built-in expects a positive integer value $n$ on the top of the stack. iota generates a vector with unit stride, starting at 0 and containing $n$ elements:

```
lang5> 5 iota .
[    0      1      2      3      4  ]
```

### 5.2.14   join

The join function is the inverse of split (see section 5.2.26) – it concatenates the elements of a vector using a glue string and thus forms a single result string which is pushed onto the stack:

```
lang5> 4 iota " plus one equals " join .
0 plus one equals 1 plus one equals 2
   plus one equals 3
```

### 5.2.15  length

The length function returns the number of elements along the
first axis of the array found in the topmost stack element. This
function does not remove the array from the stack:

```
lang5> [1 2 3] length .s
vvvvvvvvvv Begin of stack listing vvvvvvvvvv
Stack contents (TOS at bottom):
[    1    2    3  ]
3
^^^^^^^^^^ End of stack listing ^^^^^^^^^^
```

### 5.2.16  outer

outer is one of the mightiest functions in Lang5. It expects
a binary operator on the top of the stack and two vectors in
the stack elements just below. It will then create a generalized
outer "product" of these two vectors based on the operator.
The resulting type depends on the operator used. Thus a simple multiplication table can be created as follows:

```
lang5> 10 iota 1 + dup '* outer .
[
  [  1   2   3   4   5   6   7   8   9  10 ]
  [  2   4   6   8  10  12  14  16  18  20 ]
  [  3   6   9  12  15  18  21  24  27  30 ]
  [  4   8  12  16  20  24  28  32  36  40 ]
  [  5  10  15  20  25  30  35  40  45  50 ]
  [  6  12  18  24  30  36  42  48  54  60 ]
  [  7  14  21  28  35  42  49  56  63  70 ]
  [  8  16  24  32  40  48  56  64  72  80 ]
  [  9  18  27  36  45  54  63  72  81  90 ]
  [ 10  20  30  40  50  60  70  80  90 100 ]
]
```

### 5.2.17  reduce

This function also expects a binary operator in the topmost
stack element and a vector just below. It will then apply the
operator between all successive elements of the vector and
push the result of this operation back to the stack. Using

reduce the sum of the first 100 integers can be computed as
follows:

```
lang5> 100 iota 1 + '+ reduce .
5050
```

reduce always operates along the first axis of the array
to be processed, so in the following example the + operator
acts on the three one-dimensional components of the enclosing two-dimensional array:

```
lang5> [[1 2 3][4 5 6][7 8 9]] '+ reduce .
[    12     15     18   ]
```

If applied to an empty array it returns the value of the neutral element of the binary operator to which it was applied if
this operator features a neutral element. This is often useful
when dealing with boundary cases like the problem of handling the value zero in a factorial computation:

```
lang5> [] '+ reduce .
0
lang5> [] '* reduce .
1
```

> **Exercise 15:**
> Define a unary word named myfactorial to calculate the
> factorial of a positive integer value on the top of the stack.

### 5.2.18  remove

This function expects a scalar or a vector in the topmost stack
element and an array at the element just below. It will then remove all elements from the first dimension of this array which
are addressed by the elements of the vector or scalar found in
the TOS:

```
lang5> 4 iota 1 + [2 3] remove .
[    1     2   ]
lang5> [[1 2 3][4 5 6][7 8 9]] 1 remove .
[
  [    1     2     3   ]
  [    7     8     9   ]
]
```

### 5.2.19  reshape

The reshape function allows the manipulation of the structure of arrays. It expects two arrays in the two topmost stack
elements: a vector describing the structure of the resulting array, and the array the structure of which is to be changed.[3] The
following example shows how to build a three-dimensional
array based on a two dimensional vector with two times two
times two elements using reshape:

```
 1   lang5> 8 iota 1 + [2 2 2] reshape .
 2   [
 3     [
 4       [    1      2  ]
 5       [    3      4  ]
 6     ]
 7     [
 8       [    5      6  ]
 9       [    7      8  ]
10     ]
11   ]
```

If there are not enough elements in the source array to fill
the structure of the destination array, its elements are reread
from the beginning of the source array over and over again
until the result has been fully populated with values. This
behavior also applies if the source structure of the reshape
operation is a simple scalar:

```
 1   lang5> 1 [2 2] reshape .
 2   [
 3     [    1      1  ]
 4     [    1      1  ]
 5   ]
```

**Exercise 16:**

Define a unary word that expects a natural number $n$ on
the top of the stack and will create an identity matrix having $n$ columns and rows.

---

[3]Thus reshape resembles the binary case of APL's $\rho$.

## 5.2.20 `reverse`

This function reverses the elements along the first axis of an array:

```
1  lang5> [1 2 3] reverse .
2  [     3      2      1   ]
3  lang5> [[1 2] [3 4]] reverse .
4  [
5      [     3      4   ]
6      [     1      2   ]
7  ]
```

## 5.2.21 `rotate`

The `rotate` function rotates an *n*-dimensional array along any of its axes. It expects the structure to be rotated on the second to top element of the stack and a vector controlling the rotation in the topmost stack element. The following example first shows a single rotation along the first axis, followed by a rotation by -2 along the second axis and, finally, a combined rotation along both axes of a two-dimensional array:

```
1   lang5> 9 iota [3 3] reshape
2   lang5> dup [1 0] rotate .
3   [
4       [    6      7      8   ]
5       [    0      1      2   ]
6       [    3      4      5   ]
7   ]
8   lang5> dup [0 -2] rotate .
9   [
10      [    2      0      1   ]
11      [    5      3      4   ]
12      [    8      6      7   ]
13  ]
14  lang5> [1 1] rotate .
15  [
16      [    8      6      7   ]
17      [    2      0      1   ]
18      [    5      3      4   ]
19  ]
```

### 5.2.22   scatter

This function distributes (scatters) the values of a one dimensional array into a new data structure, controlled by an index vector as the following example shows:

```
lang5> ['a 'b 'c] [[0 0][0 1][1 0][1 1]] scatter .
[
   [ a b ]
   [ c a ]
]
```

As with other functions, the elements of the source array are reread from the beginning if there are not enough elements to fill the destination structure.

### 5.2.23   select

The select function selects elements from an array. It expects a one-dimensional array in the topmost stack element containing values evaluating to true (anything except 0 and the undefined value undef) or false (the value 0) and an array in the element below. The values of the control vector determine which elements from the second array are to be included in the resulting data structure:

```
lang5> ['a 'b 'c] [1 0 1] select .
[ a c ]
```

### 5.2.24   shape

shape is the inverse function to reshape – it returns a vector describing the structure of an array. This result vector contains one element for each dimension of the source data structure which has been examined, containing the number of elements along this particular axis.[4]  Obviously, applying shape twice to an array returns its dimensionality:

```
lang5> [[1 2][3 4]] shape .
[    2    2  ]
lang5> [[1 2][3 4]] shape shape .
[    2  ]
```

---

[4]Thus shape resembles the unary case of APL's $\rho$.

shape does not remove the array it operated upon from the stack.

### 5.2.25 slice

The slicefunction expects a source array on the element below the TOS and a two-element vector in the topmost stack element. This array contains two coordinate tuples controlling the slicing operation by defining an upper left and lower right "corner" of the $n$-dimensional data structure (a cube) represented by the source array. The following example shows this behavior: First, a three-dimensional cube containing 64 elements running from 0 to 63 is created. Then a sub-cube defined by the two coordinate vectors [1 1 1] and [2 2 2] is extracted from this structure and printed:

```
lang5> 64 iota [4 4 4] reshape [[1 1 1][2 2 2]]
lang5> slice .
[
  [
    [    21    22  ]
    [    25    26  ]
  ]
  [
    [    37    38  ]
    [    41    42  ]
  ]
]
```

The two-element control vector containing the coordinate tuples can also be used to slice data from a higher perspective be omitting one or more dimensions:

```
lang5> 64 iota [4 4 4] reshape [[1] [3]] slice .
[
  [
    [    16    17    18    19  ]
    [    20    21    22    23  ]
    [    24    25    26    27  ]
    [    28    29    30    31  ]
  ]
  [
    [    32    33    34    35  ]
```

```
11    [    36    37    38    39    ]
12    [    40    41    42    43    ]
13    [    44    45    46    47    ]
14  ]
15  [
16    [    48    49    50    51    ]
17    [    52    53    54    55    ]
18    [    56    57    58    59    ]
19    [    60    61    62    63    ]
20  ]
21 ]
```

Here the first two-dimensional planes from the three-dimensional 64-element cube have been sliced out.

### 5.2.26  split

The binary operator split, which is the inverse operation to join,[5] expects two scalars on the topmost stack elements: a regular expression and a string. The regular expression controls where the string is split into parts. These parts are then combined into a result array that is placed back onto the stack:

```
1  lang5> "this is a string" " " split .
2  [ this is a string ]
```

### 5.2.27  spread

The spread function applies a binary operator to the element of an array in a successive manner:

```
1  lang5> [1 2 3] '+ spread .
2  [    1     3     6   ]
```

So the first element of the result in this case is the first element of the original array, the next element of the result is the sum of the first and second elements of the source, the third element is calculated by applying the binary operator to the first three elements of the source array etc.

---

[5]See section 5.2.14.

> **Exercise 17:**
>
> Generate an array containing the squares of the first ten natural numbers without using multiplication etc. Just use spread and remember that squares can be easily generated by adding odd numbers with stride 2.

### 5.2.28  strip

The strip function removes the dress code of an array. It is the inversion function to dress:[6] If applied to a non-dressed array, nothing will happen.

```
1   lang5> [1 2](foo) strip .
2   [    1     2  ]
3   lang5> [1 2] strip .
4   [    1     2  ]
```

### 5.2.29  subscript

This function selects data from an array structure based on a vector containing coordinate vectors as the following example shows:

```
1    lang5> 64 iota [4 4 4] reshape [1 [1 1 1] [2 2 2]]
2    lang5> subscript .
3    [
4      [
5        [    16    17    18    19  ]
6        [    20    21    22    23  ]
7        [    24    25    26    27  ]
8        [    28    29    30    31  ]
9      ]
10       21    42
11   ]
```

### 5.2.30  transpose

The transpose function performs a generalized matrix transposition. It expects a control value on the top of the stack and the array to be transposed in the stack element just below:

---

[6]See section 5.2.6.

```
 1  lang5> 9 iota [3 3] reshape dup 1 transpose .s
 2  vvvvvvvvvv Begin of stack listing vvvvvvvvvv
 3  Stack contents (TOS at bottom):
 4  [
 5    [    0       1       2   ]
 6    [    3       4       5   ]
 7    [    6       7       8   ]
 8  ]
 9  [
10    [    0       3       6   ]
11    [    1       4       7   ]
12    [    2       5       8   ]
13  ]
14  ^^^^^^^^^^^ End of stack listing ^^^^^^^^^^^
```

## 5.3   File handling

The basic output functions, namely ., .., and .s have already
been used throughout the preceding examples and were described in more detail in section 5.1.  Output generated by
these functions is directed to the standard output channel,
stdout for short.

Files are referenced within Lang5 by *file numbers*. The standard handle stdout has the fixed file number 1. The functions
described in the following allow the handling of disk files.

### 5.3.1   close

This function closes a file which has been previously opened
using the open function (see section 5.3.5). close expects the
number of the file to be closed on the topmost stack element.

### 5.3.2   eof

The eof function expects the number of a previously opened
file (see section 5.3.5) on the TOS and returns the value 1 if
a following read operation (see section 5.3.6) would result in
an error due to reaching the end of the file.[7]  Otherwise 0 is
returned.

---

· [7]*EOF for short.*

### 5.3.3   fin

This function expects a valid file number in the topmost stack
element and redirects the standard input channel[8] to that particular file. All following input operations which would normally access stdin will now read from this file.

### 5.3.4   fout

The fout function redirects stdout to the file specified by the
file number in the topmost stack element.

### 5.3.5   open

This function opens a file for read, write, or append. open
expects two scalar values on the two topmost stack elements:
one describing the mode of operation for which the file will be
opened (possible values are <, >, and >> for read, write, and
append), the other one containing the name of the file.

open removes these two scalars from the stack and returns
the file number of the file just opened. The following example shows how to create a file named test.dat if it does not
already exist and write the string "Hello world!\n" to it:

```
1   lang5> '> 'test.dat open dup fout
2   lang5> "Hello world!\n" . close
```

### 5.3.6   read

read reads a record from a stream[9] and pushes it onto the
stack. Thus reading the record which was written to the file
test.dat just before can be accomplished like this:

```
1   lang5> '< 'test.dat open dup fin read . close
2   Hello world!
```

### 5.3.7   STDIN, STDOUT, STDERR

These words push the respective file numbers of the three standard IO-streams stdin, stdout and stderr[10] onto the stack.

---

[8]stdin for short. stdin has the file number 0.
[9]By default this is stdin which can be changed by fin, see section 5.3.3.
[10]The standard error stream.

### 5.3.8  unlink

The unlink function actually deletes a file whose name is specified in a string on the TOS. The following example shows how
to delete the file test.dat created in the examples above:

```
lang5> 'test.dat unlink
```

### 5.3.9  slurp

It is often quite handy to read the contents of a file in a single
step. This is accomplished by the word slurp which expects
the name of the file in the TOS element and returns a one-
dimensional array containing the records of the file. Assume
that there is a file grades.dat containing the following lines
of data:

```
Name;grade
Student a;2
Student b;5
Student c;3
Student d;1
Student e;1
```

Reading this file's contents into an array can be accomplished
like this:

```
lang5> 'grades.dat slurp .
[ Name;grade Student a;2 Student b;5 Student c;3
   Student d;1 Student e;1 ]
```

> **Exercise 18:**
>
> Define a word that expects the name of a file containing
> grades in the format shown above which reads in the file
> and returns the mean grade of all students.

## 5.4   Mathematical operations

Lang5 supports quite a lot of mathematical, logical and comparison operators and words which are described in more detail in the following. In most cases these operators and words
are rather self-explanatory.

## 5.4.1 +, -, *, /

These are the traditional binary arithmetic operations plus, minus,[11] multiplication, and division. Plus and minus have 0 as their neutral element while multiplication and division use 1 as neutral element. These four operators are already overloaded to work transparently on complex numbers which are dressed with (c). In addition to this, * has been overloaded to multiply matrices by vectors or matrices.[12]

## 5.4.2 %, **

Binary modulus and power operators. Both have 1 as their neutral element.

## 5.4.3 &, |, ^

Bit-wise and, or, and exclusive or operators.

## 5.4.4 ==, !=, >, <, >=, <=

Binary numerical comparison operators.[13] == and != are overloaded to work on complex numbers[14] as well as on polar coordinates.[15]

> **Exercise 19:**
>
> Define a word largest_only that expects two one-dimensional arrays a and b on the top of the stack and returns a one-dimensional array that only contains those elements from a that are bigger than the corresponding elements from b. Test it with two arrays [1 2 3] and [0 2 2]. The result should be the array [1 3].

## 5.4.5 ===

The binary operator === is an "exactly equals" operator. Applied to undef and 0 it will return 0 and not 1 as a simple == would do.

---

[11]Since this is a binary operator, it can not be used to change the sign of a value. To accomplish this the word neg (see section 5.4.38) is used!

[12]Matrices and vectors are dressed with (m) and (v) respectively.

[13]== and != compare for equality and inequality respectively.

[14]Dressed with (c).

[15]Dressed with (p).

### 5.4.6   eq, ne, gt, lt, ge, le

These are the string-comparison equivalents to the numerical comparison operators described in section 5.4.4.

### 5.4.7   eql

The binary string comparison operator eql is equivalent to === (see section 5.4.5), it will not treat empty strings and undef as being equal.

### 5.4.8   <=>, cmp

Generalized (alpha-)numerical comparison operators corresponding to those found in Perl. $\boxed{\text{a  b  <=>}}$ yields -1 if a is less than b, 0 if both are equal and +1 if a is greater than b. cmp behaves accordingly but the actual comparison is performed in lexicographic mode.

### 5.4.9   ||, &&

Binary logical or and and operators.

### 5.4.10   !

This unary word implements the factorial function.

### 5.4.11   ?

This so-called unary "roll" operator represents a simple pseudo-random generator. The value *n* contained in the topmost stack element is used as the upper limit for the pseudo-random number *p* to be returned which will always satisfy $0 \leq p < n$.

### 5.4.12   atan2

The binary operator atan2 returns the arc tangent function of the two topmost stack elements.

### 5.4.13   abs

The unary abs word returns the absolute value of a numerical value. In case of a complex number, dressed with (c), it will return $\sqrt{re^2 + im^2}$.

### 5.4.14 amean

This word returns the arithmetic mean of the elements in a one-dimensional vector.

**Exercise 20:**

Implement your own version of this function and call it myamean.

### 5.4.15 and

Logical and operator.

### 5.4.16 choose

choose computes the binomial coefficient of two values, i. e.

| 7 2 choose . | yields 21.

### 5.4.17 cmean

This word returns the cubic mean of the elements of a one-dimensional vector.

### 5.4.18 complex

The unary word complex converts a polar coordinate tuple (dressed with (p)) into a complex number (dressed with (c)).

### 5.4.19 corr

corr computes the PEARSON correlation coefficient of two vectors.

### 5.4.20 cos

Calls the cosine function.

### 5.4.21 defined

Returns 1 if a value is not undef. If an element is not defined, the value undef is returned:

```
1   lang5> [1 undef 2] defined 1 == .
2   [    1     0     1   ]
```

### 5.4.22 distinct

This unary word removes all elements from a set, i. e. a one-dimensional vector dressed with (s), which occur more than once:

```
lang5> [3 1 4 1 5 9 2 6 5 3 5](s) distinct .
[    1    2    3    4    5    6    9  ](s)
```

### 5.4.23 e

Places an approximation for EULER's constant onto the stack.

### 5.4.24 eps

Places a constant $\varepsilon$ onto the stack. This value should be used when comparing floating point numbers together with abs instead of a simple ==:

```
lang5> 1 3 / .3333333333333 == .
0
lang5> 1 3 / .3333333333333 - abs eps < .
1
```

### 5.4.25 exp

This unary operator returns the exponential function of the argument found in the topmost stack element.

### 5.4.26 gcd

This word expects two integer numbers in the two topmost stack elements and returns their greatest common divisor.

### 5.4.27 gmean

The word gmean returns the geometric mean of the elements of a one-dimensional vector which is expected in the TOS.

### 5.4.28 h2d

Converts a hexadecimal number (with uppercase letters) to a decimal value.

### 5.4.29  hmean

hmean returns the harmonic mean of the elements of a one-dimensional array on the TOS.

### 5.4.30  hoelder

Computes the generalized mean, the so-called HOELDER-mean of the elements of a one-dimensional array as controlled by a scalar expected on the top of the stack.

### 5.4.31  idmatrix

This word expects an integer value n on the top of stack and returns an $n \times n$ identity matrix:

```
lang5> 3 idmatrix .
[
   [    1     0     0   ]
   [    0     1     0   ]
   [    0     0     1   ]
](m)
```

### 5.4.32  im

Returns the imaginary part of a complex number (dressed with (c)):

```
lang5> [1 2](c) im .
2
```

### 5.4.33  int

This unary operator returns the integer part of a value:

```
lang5> 1 3 / int .
0
lang5> 10 [2 3 4 5] / int .
[    5     3     2     2   ]
```

### 5.4.34   intersect

This word returns the intersection of two sets (arrays dressed with (s)). Duplicate elements will be removed from the result set!

### 5.4.35   max

The binary operator max returns the maximum of two values:

```
1   lang5> 2 3 max  .
2   3
3   lang5> [1 2 3 4 5 6 7] [3 1 4 5 9 2 6] max  .
4   [    3      2      4      5      9      6      7   ]
```

**Exercise 21:**

Define a word set_max that will work on a set (dressed with s) containing numeric values which will return the maximum value of the set's elements. (Hint: You can use spread and extract to accomplish this task.)

### 5.4.36   median

This word returns the median of a one-dimensional numeric vector:

```
1   lang5> [3 1 4 5 9 2 6] median  .
2   4
```

### 5.4.37   min

This binary operator returns the minimum of two values.

### 5.4.38   neg

The unary operator neg changes the sign of a numerical value. This is necessary as minus is always treated as a binary operator and thus can not be used to change the sign of a value on the stack directly.

### 5.4.39   not

Unary not operator.

### 5.4.40 or

Binary logical or operator.

### 5.4.41 polar

This unary word converts a complex number, dressed with (c), into a polar value (dressed with (p)).

### 5.4.42 prime

This unary word tests if an integer value is a prime number and returns a positive integer if true, otherwise 0 is returned.[16]

> **Exercise 22:**
>
> Define a word prime_list that expects an integer value on the TOS and returns a list of prime numbers up to that number using the prime word.

### 5.4.43 qmean

This word returns the quadratic mean – also known as *root mean square* – of the elements of a one-dimensional array which is expected in the topmost stack element.

### 5.4.44 re

This unary word returns the real part of a complex number (dressed with (c)):

```
lang5> [1 2](c) re .
1
```

### 5.4.45 sin

Returns the sine of its argument.

### 5.4.46 sqrt

Returns the square root of a positive value.

---

[16]This word is *not* an efficient implementation of a primality test!

> **Exercise 23:**
>
> Define a new word better_sqrt that can work with positive values as well as with negative ones (returning a complex number in the latter case).

### 5.4.47  subset

This word expects two sets (dressed with (s)) on the stack and tests if the one on the TOS is a subset of the set just below. If this is true, 1 will be pushed onto the stack, 0 otherwise.

```
1   lang5> [1 2 3](s) [1 3](s) subset .
2   1
3   lang5> [1 2 3](s) [3 1 2](s) subset .
4   1
5   lang5> [1 2 3](s) [2 4](s) subset .
6   0
```

### 5.4.48  tan

This unary word returns the tangent of its argument.

### 5.4.49  union

This word expects two sets (dressed with (s)) on the stack and returns the union of these two sets. The resulting set does not contain any duplicates:

```
1   lang5> [1 2 3](s) [3 4 5](s) union .
2   [    1    2    3    4    5  ](s)
```

## 5.5  Control structures

Although the available control structures and elements have already been described in section 4.3.3 they are listed here again as a quick reference:

### 5.5.1  break

break terminates the execution of a loop which is the only way to get out of a do-loop construction. It also terminates the execution of a word when it is executed outside of a loop.

### 5.5.2 do-loop

These two keywords implement an endless loop. In contrast to Forth, Lang5 does not support an implicit loop variable like Forth's I. The only way to exit such a loop is through executing break under a certain condition.

### 5.5.3 if-else-then

These three keywords implement the traditional control structure as in other languages. Due to the stack-based nature of Lang5 if interprets the topmost element of the stack as a logical value controlling the execution of the following block of code until an else, which is optional, or the terminating then is found.

## 5.6 Miscellaneous functions and words

### 5.6.1 chr

Return the ASCII character corresponding to its argument:

```
1   lang5> 26 iota 65 + chr .
2   [ A B C D E F G H I J K L M
3     N O P Q R S T U V W X Y Z ]
```

### 5.6.2 cls

Clear screen – this word assumes a VT100 compatible terminal.

### 5.6.3 concat

Concatenate two strings:

```
1   lang5> 'abc 'def concat .
2   abcdef
```

### 5.6.4 execute

This function expects a string of Lang5-instructions or a one-dimensional array of strings of such instructions in the topmost stack element and executes these instructions:

```
1   lang5> clear "1 2 .s swap" execute .s
2   vvvvvvvvvv Begin of stack listing vvvvvvvvvv
3   Stack contents (TOS at bottom):
4   1
5   2
6   ^^^^^^^^^^ End of stack listing ^^^^^^^^^^
7   vvvvvvvvvv Begin of stack listing vvvvvvvvvv
8   Stack contents (TOS at bottom):
9   2
10  1
11  ^^^^^^^^^^ End of stack listing ^^^^^^^^^^
```

A typical application for this function is to eliminate loops with a fixed, previously known number of iterations by explicitly unrolling the loop:

```
1   lang5> "'test ." 5 reshape execute
2   testtesttesttesttest
```

### 5.6.5 exit

exit terminates the Lang5-interpreter immediately.

### 5.6.6 gplot

The gplot word is a simple interface to the gnuplot package.[17] It expects a one-dimensional array on the stack and generates a plot based on its individual elements.

### 5.6.7 help

help can be used to obtain a basic explanation of built-in functions and the like:

```
1   lang5> '+ help
2   +: Basic binary operator +, neutral element: 0.
```

### 5.6.8 lc

lc converts the string found in TOS to lower case.

---

[17]This package must be installed separately.

### 5.6.9 load

This function loads (and executes) a Lang5-program from a file. The following example shows how to execute the example program generating an ULAM-spiral which can be found in the examples-directory of the Lang5-directory tree:

```
1  lang5> 'lang5/trunk/examples/ulam.5 load
2  73                                 79
3        43                    47
4  71                    23
5        41         7
6           19              2    11         53
7                 5          3         29
8  67         17                   13
9        37                         31
10                    61         59
```

Please note that the path to the file must be enclosed in double quotes if it contains any whitespace character at all.

### 5.6.10 panic

The panic function prints the content of the topmost stack element and immediately leaves the Lang5-interpreter loop. When running in batch-mode this will terminate the Lang5-interpreter instantly, while it will just return to the command prompt when running in interactive mode.

### 5.6.11 save

The save word saves the current work-space to a file the name of which is expected in the topmost stack element. save makes use of dump (see section 5.7.4) as it loops over a list of all variable and word names and appends their respective definition to the file being written. So saving and restoring the current work-space can be done as follows:[18]

```
1  alberich$ lang5
2  loading mathlib.5: Const.. ...
3  loading stdlib.5:  Const..Misc..Stk..Struct..
```

---

[18]The -i qualifier forces the Lang5-interpreter to enter interactive mode which it would not do otherwise, if called with a file like this.

```
 4   lang5> : square dup * ;
 5
 6   lang5> 25 square .
 7   625
 8   lang5> 'my_workspace.5 save
 9   Saving workspace to my_workspace.5: done
10   lang5> exit
11
12   alberich$ lang5 -i my_workspace.5
13   loading mathlib.5: Const.. ...
14   loading stdlib.5:  Const..Misc..Stk..Struct..
15   loading my_workspace.5
16   lang5> 25 square .
17   625
18   lang5>
```

### 5.6.12   system

The unary operator executes a string at the shell level of the
operating system.[19] The results of the command executed in
the shell are placed into a one-dimensional array on the TOS:

```
 1   lang5> 'date system .
 2   [ Sun Apr  7 20:46:11 CEST 2013 ]
```

### 5.6.13   type

This function returns the type of the element in the topmost
stack element without destroying this element:

```
 1   lang5> 5 type [1 2 3] type [1 2](c) type .s
 2   vvvvvvvvvv Begin of stack listing vvvvvvvvvv
 3   Stack contents (TOS at bottom):
 4   5
 5   S
 6   [    1     2     3  ]
 7   A
 8   [    1     2  ](c)
 9   D
10   ^^^^^^^^^^ End of stack listing ^^^^^^^^^^
```

---

[19]This is a potentially very dangerous function as it will execute anything
within the context of the current user! So this feature should be used with care!

Possible results are:

B: Binary operator

U: Unary operator

N: Niladic operator

F: Built in function

V: Variable

W: User defined word

S: Scalar

A: Array

D: Dressed data structure

### 5.6.14  uc

uc converts the string found in TOS to upper case.

### 5.6.15  ver

ver pushes the version number of the Lang5-interpreter onto the stack.

## 5.7   Variable and word handling

### 5.7.1  .ofw

This built-in function prints a list of all operators, functions and words known the Lang5-interpreter at the current moment. Each name of such an element is preceded by a single character denoting its type:

B: Binary operator

U: Unary operator

N: Niladic operator

F: Built in function

V: Variable

W: User defined word

### 5.7.2  .v

This word displays a list of all defined variables, including the special variables explained in section A.

```
lang5> .v
Variables:
__log_level'      --->       'ERROR'
__number_format'          --->     '%4s'
__terminal_width'         --->     '80'
```

### 5.7.3  del

This function expects the name of a variable or user-defined word in the topmost stack element and deletes this variable or word.

### 5.7.4  dump

This function converts a user-defined word to a textual representation that is pushed as a string onto the stack.[20]

### 5.7.5  eval

This unary operator expects the name of a variable on the top of the stack and returns its content.

### 5.7.6  explain

explain expects the name of a user-defined word or variable on the topmost stack element and prints this word's or variable's definition to stdout:

```
lang5> 'prime explain
: prime(*)
  type "S" ne
  if
    "prime: TOS is not scalar!\n" panic
  then
  dup 1 ==
  if
    drop 0
```

---

[20]This function is the heart of explain.

```
10    then
11    dup 4 <
12    if
13      break
14    then
15    dup sqrt 2 / int iota 1 + 2 * 1 + [      2   ]
16    swap append % "&&" reduce
17  ;
```

### 5.7.7 set

Sets (and defines, if necessary) a variable. The name of the variable is expected in the topmost stack element and the value that variable is to be set to is expected in the stack element just below.[21]

Caution: User-defined words and variables share the same name-space, so trying to define a variable with a name already used for a user-defined word will either result in an error message if the interpreter is running in interactive mode or in an abort if the interpreter is running in batch mode!

### 5.7.8 vlist

Pushes a one-dimensional array containing the names of all variables onto the stack:

```
1  lang5> vlist .
2  [ __log_level __number_format __terminal_width ]
```

### 5.7.9 wlist

Analogous to vlist this pushes a list of the names of all user-defined words onto the stack:

```
1  lang5> wlist .
2  [ ! != * + - .s .v / 2dup == STDERR STDIN STDOUT
3    abs amean append choose clear cls cmean complex
4    corr distinct dreduce e eps explain extract gcd
5    gmean gplot h2d hmean hoelder idmatrix im
6    intersect max median min ndrop neg pi pick polar
```

---

[21]See section 4.3.6.

```
prime qmean re roll rot save slurp subset tan
union ]
```

# Chapter 6

# Programming examples

The following sections contain some introductory Lang5 programming examples which range from rather simple to quite complex and sometimes even tricky. Each program should be seen as an invitation for dissecting it and experimenting with alternative solutions.

## 6.1 Fibonacci numbers

The elements of the sequence defined by

$$f(0) = (1) = 1 \text{ and}$$
$$f(i) = f(i-1) + f(i-2) \ \forall i > 1$$

are called FIBONACCI *numbers* in honor of LEONARDO PISANO who discovered this sequence.[1] This sequence can be recursively generated with Lang5 like this:[2]

```
1  : fib              # Define a word named fib
2      dup 2 <        # Handle first
3      if             # two sequence
4          drop 1     # elements.
5      else           # All other
6          dup        # elements end
7          1 - fib    # here.
8          swap 2 - fib
```

---

[1] See [LÜNEBURG 1993].

[2] Remember that, as in Perl, there is (always) more than one way to do it!

83

```
9              +
10        then
11    ;
12
13    0 do # Make a loop running from 0 to 10.
14        dup fib .   1 +
15        dup 10 > if break then
16    loop
```

As straightforward as this solution is, it makes no use of
any Lang5 features exceeding those of a traditional Forth interpreter. Defining a unary word fib(*) the explicit loop can
be replaced by applying this word to a vector with unit stride
as the following program shows:

```
1    : fib(*)
2      dup 2 < if drop 1 break then
3      dup 1 - fib swap 2 - fib +
4    ;
5
6    10 iota fib .
```

## 6.2   Throwing dice

More of the array language features of Lang5 are employed
in the following example in which the arithmetic mean of the
outcomes of throwing a six sided die $n \in \mathbb{N}$ times is computed.
Whereas non-array languages would require a loop to perform
the repeated throwing of the die this is accomplished in Lang5
by first creating a vector containing $n$ times the value 6 representing the number of sides of the die. Such a vector containing 100 elements can be created by $\boxed{6\ 100\ \text{reshape}}$

Applying the unary ? operator to this vector will consume
this vector and generate a new vector containing 100 pseudo-
random numbers $0 \leq r < 6$. Since a die always yields a natural
number between 1 and 6, the unary int operator will be applied to this vector, truncating every floating point vector element. Adding one finally yields the desired vector containing
100 elements between 1 and 6.

In the last step, these vector's elements are summed by `'+ reduce` and then divided by the number of elements to return the desired arithmetic mean. The following listing contains a complete Lang5 program implementing this example:

```
 1  : throw_dice
 2    # Make a vector of the form [6 6 6 ... 6].
 3    6 over reshape
 4
 5    #  Throw dice n times, retain integer part and
 6    # make sure the results are between 1 and 6.
 7    ? int 1 +
 8
 9    #  Sum over all results and divide by the
10    # number of values.
11    '+ reduce swap /
12  ;
13
14  100 throw_dice .
```

## 6.3 Cosine approximation

Applying the very same principles, a simple cosine approximation using the well known MacLaurin series

$$\cos x \approx \sum_{i=0}^{n} (-1)^i \frac{x^{2i}}{(2i)!}$$

can be written in Lang5 without any explicit loops at all as the following example shows:

```
 1  #
 2  #  Approximation of the cosine function using a
 3  # MacLaurin series of 11 terms. The argument is
 4  # expected on the TOS.
 5  #
 6  : mc_cos
 7      #  Save x and the number of MacLaurin terms
 8      # for future use.
 9      'x set 9 'terms set
10
11      # Generate a vector containing x ** (2 * i).
```

```
12     terms iota dup defined x * swap 2 * dup
13     'v2i set **
14
15     #  Generate a vector containing (2 * i)! and
16     # divide the previous vector.
17     v2i ! /
18
19     #  Generate a vector of the form
20     # [1 -1 1 -1 1 ...].
21     terms iota 1 + 2 % 2 * 1 -
22
23     #  Multiply both vectors and compute the sum
24     # of the result's elements.
25     * '+ reduce
26  ;
27
28  3.14159265 mc_cos .
```

## 6.4   List of primes

A typical way to generate a list of primes in an array language such as APL has already been shown in section 1.2:

$$(\sim E \in E \circ . \times E)/E \leftarrow 1 \downarrow \iota E \leftarrow 100$$

This APL expression generates a vector with unit stride, starting with 2 and uses this as the base for creating a matrix by applying an outer product operation. This matrix contains no prime numbers at all and can thus be used to select all values from a copy of this vector which are not contained in the matrix thus yielding a list of prime numbers. Its equivalent Lang5-implementation looks like this:

```
1  : prime_list
2    1 - iota 2 +   # Generate a vector [2 .. TOS].
3    dup dup dup    # Make sure there are four
4                   # identical vectors.
5    '* outer       # Outer product of the top two
6                   # vectors.
7    swap in        # Generate a selection vector
8                   # based on vector and matrix.
9    not            # Invert the elements of this
```

```
10                     # vector.
11    select           # Use this vector to select
12                     # elements from the vector
13                     # [2 .. TOS].
14    ;
15
16    do
17      "Please enter a number between 2 and 100: " .
18      read
19      dup 2 < if
20        "\tToo small!\n" . drop
21      else
22        dup 100 > if
23          "\tToo large!\n" . drop
24        else
25          break
26        then
27      then
28    loop
29
30    prime_list .
```

**Exercise 24:**

Implement a unary word called myprime that returns 0 for a non-prime argument and 1 otherwise. This word should rely on trial divisions using the modulus operation without any explicit loop or conditional. To test if a given $n \in \mathbb{N}$ is prime, a vector containing $\sqrt{n} - 1$ elements $n$ could generated in a first step. Then a vector with divisors might be generated and both vectors could be processed by %. If there is any value that divides $n$ without remainder, $n$ is obviously not prime.

## 6.5 Printing a sine curve

Generating simple ASCII plots of functions is easy in an array language like Lang5. The basic idea is to mimic a strip chart recorder. Each line printed corresponds to one $x$-coordinate. The $y$-coordinate of a point to be printed is then set by generating a string of as many spaces as specified by the value of the $y$-coordinate.

```
1   #   Generate a string consisting of n (from TOS)
2   # "-" and terminated # by CR/LF.
3   : print_dot(*)
4       " " 1 compress swap reshape "*\n" append
5       "" join .
6   ;
7
8   #   Create a vector containing the width of the
9   # bargraph to be printed.
10  21 iota 10 / 3.14159265 * sin 20 * 25 + int
11
12  print_dot # Apply the word print_bar elementwise
13             # to this vector.
```

The output generated by this program has already been shown in section 3.3.

## 6.6   Sorting external data

This example is just a variation of exercise number 18:

```
1   a ; 7
2   b ; 1
3   c ; 3
```

```
1   : get_upper(*) '; split expand drop swap drop ;
2   : get_lower(*) '; split expand drop drop ;
3
4   'sort.data slurp dup
5   get_lower swap get_upper
6   grade swap drop subscript
7   .
```

## 6.7   Matrix-vector-multiplication

Since the basic built-in multiplication operator * only performs an element-wise multiplication of two data structures, it must be explicitly overloaded to perform a matrix-vector-multiplication:

```
1   # Multiplication word:
2   : *(m,v)
3     # Calculate the inner sum of a vector:
4     : inner+(*) '+ reduce ;
5
6     # Get rid of the dress codes:
7     strip swap strip swap
8
9     * 'inner+ apply
10    'v dress
11  ;
12
13  #  Create a 3-by-3 matrix and a three-element
14  # vector:
15  9 iota 1 + [3 3] reshape 'm dress
16  3 iota 10 + 'v dress
17
18  # Multiply the matrix with the vector:
19  * .
```

The definition :  *(m,v) ...; overloads the multiplication operator for matrix-vector-operations. First a unary local
word inner+ which computes the sum of the elements of a
vector is defined before the dress codes of the arguments for
this multiplication operator are stripped.

The multiplication performed in the following step is the
basic multiplication which will work in an element-wise fashion on the elements of the two- and the one-dimensional data
structure. The resulting two-dimensional matrix is then re-
duced to a vector by applying inner+. Dressing it as a vector
completes the operation.

## 6.8  Sum of cubes

[ADAMS et al. 2009][p. 41] contains a short FORTRAN example
program which generates a list of all natural numbers between
100 and 999 which are equal to the sum of the cubes of their
respective digits. The approach taken in this program is pretty
straight-forward: Three nested loops generate the three digits of the numbers to be tested.  The number made up from

these digits is then compared to the sum of the digit cubes
and printed if both are equal.

```
1   program sum_of_cubes
2   ! This program prints all 3-digit-numbers that
3   ! equal the sum of the cubes of their digits.
4   implicit none
5   integer :: H, T, U
6   do H = 1, 9
7     do T = 0, 9
8       do U = 0, 9
9         if ( 100*H+10*T+U == H**3+T**3+U**3) &
10           print "(3I1)", H, T, U
11      end do
12    end do
13  end do
```

Using an array language the same problem can be solved
much more elegantly:

```
1   #  Print all natural numbers < 1000 which are
2   #  equal to the sum of the cubes of their
3   #  respective digits:
4
5   : cube_sum(*) "" split 3 ** '+ reduce ;
6   900 iota 100 + dup dup cube_sum == select .
```

$\boxed{\text{999 iota 1 +}}$ generates an array containing all numbers
to be tested. After creating a couple of copies of this vector,
the unary word cube_sum is applied to this array. This word
splits a number on an empty string which results in an array containing the individual digits of this number.[3] These
digits are then taken to their third power and summed using
reduce. The array resulting from applying cube_sum to the
original value array is then compared with one of the copies
for equality yielding a binary selection vector. Using select
only those elements which are equal to their digit-cube-sum
are selected and printed.

---

[3]It should be noted that a number is automatically treated as a string in this
context.

## 6.9 Perfect numbers

A so-called *perfect number* is a natural number which is equal
to the sum of its positive divisors excluding the number it-
self. Using $\boxed{\text{\% not}}$ in the unary word p the divisors of a given
natural number are identified by creating a vector containing
1 at the position of every divisor and 0 in all other places.
This array is then used to generate a list of the divisors by
select which is then summed and compared to the value being tested:

```
1   : p(*)
2     dup dup 1 - iota 1 + dup rot swap
3     % not select '+ reduce ==
4   ;
5   500 iota 1 + dup p select .
```

### 6.10 MANDELBROT set

The so-called MANDELBROT *set* which was discovered by BENOIT
MANDELBROT is the archetypal fractal shape. It is generated by
successive application of the iteration

$$z_{n+1} = z_n^2 + c \tag{6.1}$$

to the points of a grid on the complex number plane where $c$
represents the individual grid points. This sequence diverges
for a given $c$ if it exceeds the absolute value 2.

Normally the values $c$ to be considered are generated by
two nested loops covering the area of the complex plane in
question. Then (6.1) would be applied to each $c$ in a third loop
until it either diverges or until a maximum number of iterations has been reached. The number of iterations this last loop
performed until it terminates is then used to select a color denoting the behavior of this particular $c$ (divergent or possibly
convergent).

Obviously, a Mandelbrot set can be generated without any
explicit loops in an array language. The program shown in the
following first defines three words: d2c takes two scalar values
and creates a complex number by compressing and dressing
the resulting array.

iterate is a unary word expecting a complex number as its argument. This word performs the actual iterations without any explicit loop at all: The basic iteration step is defined as a string $\boxed{\text{dup * over +}}$ which is then repeatedly stored into an array using reshape. This array is then executed as a Lang5-program.[4] The third word, print_line prints one single line of the Mandelbrot set: The value generated by applying (6.1) to every $c$ is used to select one character out of a string containing a number of characters of decreasing optical density. The main program sets up a two-dimensional array of complex numbers on which iterate operates.

```
 1   # Make a complex number.
 2   : d2c(*,*) 2 compress 'c dress ;
 3
 4   : iterate(c) [0 0](c)
 5     "dup * over +" steps reshape execute
 6   ;
 7
 8   : print_line(*)
 9     "#*+-. " "" split swap subscript
10     "" join . "\n" .
11   ;
12
13   75 iota 45 - 20 / # x coordinates
14   29 iota 14 - 10 / # y cordinates
15   'd2c outer          # Make complex matrix.
16
17   10 'steps set       # How many iterations?
18
19   iterate abs int 5 min
20   'print_line apply # Compute & print.
```

This program yields the following output:

```
alberich$ lang5 apple.5
loading mathlib.5: Const.. ...
loading stdlib.5:  Const..Misc..Stk..Struct..
loading apple.5
```

---

[4]Effectively this closely resembles the process of *loop unrolling* performed by optimizers in most compilers.

```
                          #
                         *  **
                         ##*
                        *#####
                       +*####*-            *
                     *##############*#*#*
                     #*##################
        *          *####################-*
       -##*###*..*#####################
       *##############################
      *################################
+*#*#*#*#**##################################*
       *###############################
        *#############################
       -##*###*..*#####################
        *          *###################-*
                   #*##################
                    *##############*#*#*
                      +*####*-        *
                       *#####
                        ##*
                        *  **
                          #
```

## 6.11 Game of Life

In 1970, the British mathematician JOHN HORTON CONWAY developed a two-dimensional cellular automaton based on four simple rules which should become the icon of a decade. This automaton consists of cells on a toroidal surface. Each such cell is connected to its eight direct neighbors. A cell is in one of two states at every moment: *alive* or *dead* as determined by the following set of rules:

1. A cell being alive dies if it has fewer than two living neighbor cells.

2. It also dies if there are more than three neighbor cells being alive.

3. A dead cell will change its state to alive when it has exactly three neighbor cells which are alive.

4. A living cell continues to live if it has two or three living neighbor cells.

The main program shown below makes extensive use of the loop unrolling trick shown in the preceding section 6.10 by creating an instruction array containing elements of the form print_field iterate and executing these instructions. The word print_field prints the field of cells while iterate performs one actual iteration of the cellular automaton.

The number of neighbor cells being alive is determined by a trick: The current state of the automaton which is represented by a two-dimensional array is copied eight times. Each of these copies is then rotated by ±1 horizontally, vertically and diagonally.

The state of a cell is represented by the values 0 and 1 for the states *dead* and *alive* respectively. Summing these eight matrices yields the number of neighbor cells being alive. This value is then used to determine the new state of every cell by applying the locally defined binary word rule which implements the rule set shown above.

```
1   #
2   #  This is a 5-implementation of Conway's
3   # Game-of-Life.
4   #
5   #  The idea is to create eight matrices, based on
6   # the Game-of-Life matrix, where a 1 denotes a
7   # living cell while a 0 denotes a dead cell. These
8   # eight matrices are the result of eight matrix
9   # rotations (left, right, up, down, upper left,
10  # upper right, lower left, lower right).
11  #  These eight matrices are then summed to deter-
12  # mine the number of neighbours of each cell.
13  # After that the standard Game-of-Life-rules are
14  # applied to the original matrix and the neighbour
15  # sum matrix to determine the new population.
16  #
17
18  # Pretty print the field of cells with a frame.
19  : print_field
```

```
20    : print_line(*)
21        [" " "*"] swap subscript
22        "" join '! . . '! . "\n" .
23      ;
24
25      dup shape expand drop swap drop 2 + '- swap
26      reshape "" join dup . "\n" .
27      swap 'print_line apply drop . "\n" .
28    ;
29
30    : iterate # Perform one Game-of-Life-iteration.
31      : rule(*,*)
32        swap if dup 2 >= swap 3 <= && else 3 == then
33      ;
34
35      #  Rotate the matrix in all eight directions
36      # and sum these eight matrices:
37      dup [1 0]    rotate swap
38      dup [-1 0]   rotate swap
39      dup [0 1]    rotate swap
40      dup [0 -1]   rotate swap
41      dup [1 1]    rotate swap
42      dup [-1 1]   rotate swap
43      dup [1 -1]   rotate swap
44      dup [-1 -1]  rotate swap
45
46      9 -1 _roll + + + + + + + rule
47    ;
48
49    : create_matrix(*) "" split " " ne ;
50
51    #  Setup the start matrix - in this case it
52    # contains a glider:
53    [
54        "                        "
55        "                        "
56        "                        "
57        "          *             "
58        "           *            "
59        "         ***            "
60        "                        "
61        "                        "
```

```
62        "                    "
63     ]
64
65     # Perform 100 iterations:
66     create_matrix "print_field iterate" 100 reshape
67     execute
```

The start configuration defined in the program shown above is the so-called *glider*. This cell configuration exhibits a noteworthy repetitive pattern and slowly moves through the living space of the automaton:[5]

```
------------------        ------------------
!                !        !                !
!                !        !                !
!                !        !                !
!      *         !        !                !
!        *       !        !      *   *     !
!      * * *     !        !        * *     !
!                !        !        *       !
!                !        !                !
!                !        !                !
!                !        !                !
------------------        ------------------
```

```
------------------        ------------------
!                !        !                !
!                !        !                !
!                !        !                !
!                !        !                !
!        *       !        !        *       !
!      *   *     !        !          * *   !
!        * *     !        !        * *     !
!                !        !                !
!                !        !                !
!                !        !                !
------------------        ------------------
```

---

[5]It should be noted that the *Game-of-life* cellular automaton has been shown to be Turing complete, i.e. it is as powerful as a universal Turing machine from a computational point of view.

## 6.12 ULAM spiral

The so-called ULAM *spiral* is a simple yet interesting way to visualize the distribution of prime numbers. The idea is simple: Generate a rectangular spiral of natural numbers, starting with 2 in the middle. Then leave out the places of non-prime numbers so that only the prime numbers remain. The resulting structure shows intriguing patterns which are connected to polynomials generating rather long sequences of prime numbers.

The following program is a bit more tricky than the examples shown before. Figuring out its operation is left as an exercise to the reader.

```
: ulam_spiral
  : seq
    : zip(*,*) 2 compress " " join ;
    : subsubseq swap 2 2 compress reshape ;
    : subseq
      0 pick      [0 1]   subsubseq
      1 pick      [1 0]   subsubseq
      2 pick 1 + [0 -1] subsubseq
      3 pick 1 + [-1 0] subsubseq
      5 roll drop append append append
    ;

    dup 2 reshape 1 compress
    over iota 2 * 1 + "subseq append" 3 pick
    reshape zip execute over 2 * [0 1]
    subsubseq append '+ spread
  ;

  : print_line(*)
    : rpl(*) dup not if drop "" then ;
    rpl "\t" join . "\n" .
  ;

  seq swap 2 * 1 + 2 ** iota 1 + dup prime swap
  and swap scatter 'print_line apply drop
;

4 ulam_spiral
```

The output of the program shown above is too small to show the patterns of mostly diagonal lines containing prime numbers, but it shows the basic form of such a ULAM spiral:

```
alberich$ lang5 ulam.5
loading mathlib.5: Const.. ...
loading stdlib.5:  Const..Misc..Stk..Struct..
loading ulam.5
73                                    79
    43                      47
71                      23
    41          7
          19              2   11            53
              5           3           29
67          17                13
    37                              31
                    61          59
```

# Chapter 7

# Exercises

## 7.1 Number bases

Develop Lang5-words that transform numerical values from one base to another (h2d just serves a special case, converting from base 16 to base 10). Bases should range from 2 (yielding a binary representation) to 36 (using the digits 0 to 9 and the characters A to Z).

## 7.2 Fractions

Write a Lang5-library called frac.5 which implements all necessary words to deal with data structures dressed as fraction representing fractions. This library should overload the basic arithmetic operators +, -, *, and /. It should implement explicit and implicit reduction of a fraction etc.

## 7.3 Regression

Implement a Lang5-word that computes a linear regression for a given set of data.

## 7.4 Matrices

Extend the matrix/vector capabilities of the standard Lang5-libraries by developing and adding words to compute the determinant, the inverse of a matrix etc.

# Chapter 8

# Interpreter anatomy

The following sections provide a short walk-through of the Lang5-interpreter's source code. This is by no means a thorough description of every implementation detail, it is intended to serve as a starting point for a more thorough evaluation by the reader.

## 8.1 The wrapper lang5

The Lang5-interpreter itself is fully encapsulated in the Perl module Lang5.pm while the actual user-interface is implemented in the file lang5 which can be found in the main directory of the interpreter directory tree. First of all, a Lang5-object is instantiated like this:

```
1   my $fip = Lang5->new(
2       log_level       => $opt{debug_level},
3       number_format   => $opt{format},
4       text_callback   => sub {
5           $line_count += tr/\n/\n/ for @_;
6           print $OUT @_;
7       },
8       libdir          => "$Bin/lib",
9       libautoload     => !$opt{nolibs},
10  );
```

All of the interpreter's functionality can now be accessed via $fip. In the next step a signal handler for catching SIGINT is registered and the current system time is stored (required for measuring execution times).

The interpreter can operate in three modes which are partially mutually exclusive:

**Evaluating code specified on the command line:** A program which is included in double quotes following the -e qualifier is executed immediately. This is controlled by the command line parameter contained in the hash-element $opt{evaluate} which reflects -e.

**Batch mode:** If any source files are specified on the command line their contents will be read and executed by the interpreter. This is done by looping over the contents of ARGV which no longer contain any qualifiers and other parameters since these have already been removed by GetOptions.

**Interactive mode:** This mode is mutually exclusive with the -e option. In interactive mode, commands are read from the standard input using readline.

In any of these three cases, a Lang5-program is executed by calling the subroutine execute which expects a reference to the Lang5-object, a reference to an array containing the lines of source to be executed, and a handle for output operations. It then performs the following actions:

```
1   $fip->add_source_line($_)  # Build a program from
2       for @$lines;           # the individual lines.
3   $fip->execute();           # Execute the program.
4   if ( $fip->error() ) {     # Handle any errors
5       ...                    # which may have
6                              # occurred.
7   }
```

The remaining parts of lang5 mostly deal with handling statistical data and printing a usage summary if the program has been called with invalid options.

The following sections are focused on the Lang5-interpreter contained in perl_modules/Lang5.pm.

## 8.2 Parsing

The first stage of execution of a Lang5-program is to build a nested data structure representing the program in a form that makes it possible for the interpreter to execute the individual program statements.

The method add_source_line is called for every single line of source code. It skips empty lines and gets rid of invalid characters. (The latter are normally caused by sloppy typing such as holding the ALT key for too long after typing a closing square bracket, which makes a single space character become an ALT-space.) Other valid characters like single quotes, double quotes and quoted backslashes are escaped by replacing them by constants like _CTSQ_. This simplifies the following tasks of the parser.

Special treatment is necessary for word headers consisting of an initial colon and a word name with optional parentheses. The central hash %re contains some regular expressions which are used throughout the interpreter – one of these expressions is used to determine the start of a word definition:

```
1  my %re = (
2    float => qr/^([+-]?)(?=\d|\.\d)\d*(\.\d*)?
3      ([Ee]([+-]?\d+))?$/,
4    whead => qr/\S+\{\[.+?\}/,
5    strob => qr/\Qbless( do{\(my \E\$o = ('.*')\Q)},
6              'Lang5::String' )/,
7  );
```

The regular expression stored in the entry float matches a floating point number, the expression stored in whead has been mentioned above, and strob contains a regular expression which is used to detect Lang5::String objects.

Since keywords in Lang5-source code are mainly separated by white-space, it is necessary to protect strings which might contain white-spaces from being erroneously split into parts. This is done using the function _secure_string. After removing comments, the line processed like this is finally appended to an array referenced by $self->{_line_buffer}.

To get an impression of the preprocessing operations performed by the subroutine add_source_line the following short example program is considered:

```
1   : loop_exa
2     1 do dup . 1 + dup 5 > if break then loop
3   ;
4
5   loop_exa "Loop finished. Print array:" .
6   [[1 2] [3 4]] .
```

After processing the individual lines of this program by means of the function add_source_line the buffer hash-entry $self->{_line_buffer} contains the following data:[1]

```
$1 = [
  ': loop_exa',
  '  1 do dup . 1 + dup 5 > if break then loop ',
  ';',
  'loop_exa{4c6f6f702066696e69736865642e204
                    e6f772 07072696e7420616e2061727
                    261793a}  .',
  '[[1 2] [3 4]] .'
];
```

After all lines of a Lang5-program are processed in this fashion, the method execute is called which in turn calls the subroutine _parse_source. This function splits the lines contained in $self->{_line_buffer} on white-space and square brackets. Applied to the example program above, the result of this call is a data structure of the following form:

```
$1 = [
  ':',
  'loop_example',
  '1',
  'do',
  'dup',
  '.',
  '1',
  '+',
  'dup',
  '5',
  '>',
```

---

[1] Printed with Data::Dumper.

```
  'if',
  'break',
  'then',
  'loop',
  ';',
  'loop_example',
  bless(do{\(my $o='Loop finished. Print array:')},
            'Lang5::String' ),
  '.',
  '[',
  '[',
  '1',
  '2',
  ']',
  '[',
  '3',
  '4',
  ']',
  ']',
  '.'
];
```

Clearly, since this process of splitting the source into a stream of tokens just returned a sequence of square brackets and values, the two-dimensional array to be printed at the end of the example program needs some further processing to produce an array for the next stage. This is done in _transmogrify_arrays. Applied to the data structure shown above it returns this:

```
$1 = [
  ':',
  'loop_example',
  '1',
...
  '.',
  [
    [
       '1',
       '2'
    ],
    [
```

```
      '3',
      '4'
    ]
  ],
  '.'
];
```

The array specified as [[1 2][3 4]] in the source code
is now represented by a true two-dimensional array. The next
part of the parser handles structures like if...else...then
and do...loop. This is done by calling _if_do_structures
which transforms the data structure representing the example
into this:

```
$1 = [
  ':',
  'loop_example',
  '1',
  'do',
  [
    'dup',
    '.',
    '1',
    '+',
    'dup',
    '5',
    '>',
    'if',
    [
      'break'
    ]
  ],
  ';',
  'loop_example',
  bless(do{\(my $o='Loop finished. Print array:')},
          'Lang5::String' ),
  '.',
  [
    [
      '1',
      '2'
    ],
```

```
    [
        '3',
        '4'
    ]
  ],
  '.'
];
```

The program's structure is now represented by a nested data structure which is then used as input to the central interpreter routine _execute.

## 8.3  _execute

_execute is the heart of the interpreter. It acts on a data structure like that shown above and effectively executes a program by traversing this structure. It is implemented as a finite-state machine with the following states:

```
 1  use constant {
 2      STATE_RUN                   => 0,
 3      STATE_START_WORD            => 1,
 4      STATE_EXPAND_WORD           => 2,
 5      STATE_SKIP_WORD_DEFINITION  => 3,
 6      STATE_EXECUTE_IF            => 4,
 7      STATE_EXECUTE_ELSE          => 5,
 8      STATE_IF_COMPLETED          => 6,
 9      STATE_EXECUTE_DO            => 7,
10      STATE_BREAK_EXECUTED        => 8,
11  };
```

Beginning with the initial state STATE_RUN, _execute loops over the elements of the array containing the preprocessed and parsed program. _execute calls itself recursively whenever a nested program part controlled by a conditional or a loop is encountered.

## 8.4   Built-ins etc.

_execute relies on a nested data structure quite similar to that shown in the simple RPN parser of section 2.1. This structure is contained in a hash %builtin and basically looks like this:

```perl
my %builtin = (

  ### niladic operators
  exit  => {
    desc => 'Leave the interpreter immediately.',
    type => 'niladic',
    code => sub { $_[0]->{_exit_called} = 1; },
  },
...
  ### unary operators
  '?' => {
    desc => 'Generate a pseudo random number.',
    type => 'unary',
    pop  => [qw/X/],
    push => [qw/I/],
    ntrl => 0,
    code => sub { rand($_[1]); },
  },
...
  ### binary operators
  # direct mapping to perl operators
  # with 0 as neutral element
  ( map {
    $_ => {
      desc => "Basic bin. operator $_, ntrl: 0.",
      type => 'binary',
      pop  => [qw/X X/],
      push => [qw/S/],
      ntrl => 0,
      code => eval("sub { no warnings qw/numeric/;
      \$_[2] $_ \$_[1] }"),
    }
  } qw(
    + -
  )),
...
```

Every built-in operator/function is represented by an entry in this hash which references a nested hash containing the following keys:

desc: This entry contains an optional short help text describing the operation itself.[2]

type: Every language element is of a specific type which is stored in this entry. Possible values are: niladic, unary, binary, function, and variable.[3]

pop: This entry describes how many values are popped from the stack by an operation and the expected type of these values. Possible values are:

A: Array

BO: Binary operator

I: Integer value

F: Floating point value

PI: Positive integer value

V: A valid variable name

S: Any scalar value

X: Any value

U: A user defined word

N: A name of a user defined word or variable

These values are used for automatic checks of the values before executing a built-in. Central element for this type checking is the dispatch table %param_checks which maps these type descriptors to check functions.

push: This describes what will be pushed back onto the stack.[4]

ntrl: Value of the neutral element which will be returned if one of the arguments of the operator/function is undefined.

code: The actual functionality of the built-in.

Since unary and binary operations are automatically applied in an element-wise fashion onto nested data structures, the interpreter core _execute relies on two subroutines _unary and _binary which in turn call unary and binary from the Perl module Array::DeepUtils which contains the (rather complicated) array handling capabilities.

---

[2]See section 5.6.7.

[3]These types are normally referred in the source code by their first letter only.

[4]This information is not currently used by the interpreter.

## 8.5 Stacks

The central data structure of any Lang5-program is the stack onto which all operands have to be placed before they can be processed. Pushing a value onto the stack is straight-forward in case of a scalar: `push $stack, $element + 0;`

When an array is to be pushed onto the stack, things are a bit more complicated. A simple `push $stack, $element` would push a reference to the array onto the stack. If this array was in turn read from a variable this would have the effect that any change on the array on the stack would affect the value of the variable through the reference![5] To avoid this problem, any nested data structure which is to be pushed onto the stack is first copied using dclone. from Array::DeepUtils.

## 8.6 Local stacks

Although in theory all operators, functions and words could operate on a single central stack, this would pose the risk of changing values on the central stack by side-effects. To avoid this the Lang5-interpreter creates a local stack every time an operation is to be performed. In the case of a unary or binary operation, one or two values are fetched from the central stack and pushed onto this temporary stack on which the operation to be executed itself acts.

Whatever will be found in the top-most stack element of such a local stack after the execution of the operator or the like has finished will be pushed onto the central stack and the local stack will be destroyed.

## 8.7 Questions

> **Exercise 25:**
>
> Draw a state diagram of _execute. Note that the sequence of the conditionals which control the state transitions in the source code is essential for correct operation (explain why).

---

[5]In fact, this was a bug in the interpreter which was only detected and corrected recently (after more than two years of development).

**Exercise 26:**

Follow the operation of the Lang5-interpreter by executing a simple program without loading the standard libraries (this is to simplify things – the definitions in the library are plenty and many of them are rather complex) by specifying the -n qualifier. To trace the operation of the interpreter specify -d TRACE on the command line.

**Exercise 27:**

Analyze the structure which results from a user defined word. To do so, follow the program flow starting with the state STATE_START_WORD of the finite-state machine in _execute.

**Exercise 28:**

Explore how overloading user defined words actually works. Central to this functionality is the subroutine _get_func.

**Exercise 29:**

Why isn't it necessary to use dclone when pushing the arguments onto the local stack for an unary or binary operator? Why does pushing a reference suffice and not cause unwanted side effects?

## Chapter 9

# Extending Perl

All of the nice array-handling functionality of Lang5 is also available within the Perl environment by means of the module Array::APX which overloads some of the built-in operators of Perl and introduces some useful methods for dealing with nested data structures. This module is basically a wrapper around Array::DeepUtils.[1]

The following example shows how the element-wise product of two vectors can be computed using this module:

```
1   use strict;
2   use warnings;
3   use Array::APX qw(:all);
4
5   # Create two vectors [1 2 3] and [4 5 6]:
6   my $x = iota(3) + 1;
7   my $y = iota(3) + 4;
8
9   # Multiply both vectors and print the result:
10  print $x * $y;
```

A noteworthy feature of Array::APX is that some of Perl's standard operators are not only overloaded to operate on APX-objects but also act as reduce operator or as outer product. The reduce operator is represented by / as in APL:

---

[1] Array::APX was introduced at the YAPC::Europe 2012, see [ULMANN 2012]. The source of this module can be found at http://cpansearch.perl.org/src/VAXMAN/Array-APX-0.6/lib/Array/APX.pm.

113

```
1   use strict;
2   use warnings;
3   use Array::APX qw(:all);
4
5   # Create a vector [1 .. 100]:
6   my $x = iota(100) + 1;
7
8   my $adder = sub {$_[0] + $_[1]};
9   print 'The sum of all elements is ',
10      $adder / $x, "\n";
```

Outer products are specified by enclosing a binary operator which in fact is a reference to a suitable subroutine in pipe
symbols:

```
1   use strict;
2   use warnings;
3   use Array::APX qw(:all);
4
5   my $x = iota(10) + 1;
6   my $m = sub {$_[0] * $_[1]};
7
8   print $x |$m| $x;
```

Implementing the algorithm for generating a list of primes
shown in section 1.2 using Array::APX is straight-forward:

```
1   use strict;
2   use warnings;
3   use Array::APX qw(:all);
4
5   # We need an outer product
6   my $f = sub { $_[0] * $_[1] };
7   my $x;
8
9   print $x->select(!($x=iota(199)+2)->in($x|$f|$x));
```

The Array::APX module is listed in appendix D.

# Appendix A

# Special purpose variables

There are a couple of variables that control the operation of the Lang5-interpreter. These variables can be set during run time like other variables which will affect the interpreter's behavior accordingly. Currently the following special variables are supported:

__log_level:__ Normally this variable will be set to "ERROR" causing the interpreter to log error messages only. Possible values for this special variable are "TRACE", "DEBUG", "INFO", "WARN", "ERROR", and "FATAL". This variable should not be changed unless one really needs to get more information about the operation of the interpreter. Especially the settings "DEBUG" and "INFO" will generate substantial amounts of output rendering normal operation more or less impossible. These are useful only for debugging the interpreter itself.

__number_format:__ The main function to print values, ., uses the format description found in this variable for printing scalar values. By default this variable is set to "%4s".

__terminal_width:__ Some functions (like dump) need to know about the size of the terminal being used which is specified using this special variable.

# Appendix B

# The standard library

```
###
### stdlib.5, the standard library for 5.
###
### Internal variables are always prefixed by '_<word>' to avoid collisions
### between different words.
###

"loading stdlib.5:  " .

#======================================================================
"Const.." .
: STDIN  0 ;
: STDOUT 1 ;
: STDERR 2 ;

#======================================================================
"Misc.." . # Housekeeping words.

# Stack pretty printer (non-desctructive).
: .s
  depth 0 == if "Stack is empty!\n" . break then
  "vvvvvvvvvvvvvvvvvvvvv Begin of stack listing vvvvvvvvvvvvvvvvvvvvvv\n" .
  "Stack contents (TOS at bottom):\n" .
  depth compress dup
  do
    length 0 == if break then
    0 extract .
  loop
  drop expand drop
  "\n^^^^^^^^^^^^^^^^^^^^^ End of stack listing ^^^^^^^^^^^^^^^^^^^^^^\n" .
;

# Print a list of all variables known to the interpreter.
: .v
  "Variables:\n" .
  vlist                         # Get list of all variable names.
  do                            # Process the list.
    length 0 == if break then   # Anything left to print?
    0 extract                   # Get name to be printed.
    dup "\t--->\t"              # Prepare string to be printed.
    rot eval                    # Get value of variable.
    "\n" 4 compress "'" join .  # Make string and print line.
```

117

```
  loop drop
;

# CLear Screen (assuming a VT100 terminal):
: cls 27 chr "[2J" 27 chr "[;H" 4 compress "" join . ;

# explain a word.
: explain dump . ;

# Save the current workspace - expects destination filename on TOS.
: save
  : uxplain(*) explain ;

  depth 1 < if "save: Not enough elements on stack!\n" panic then
  type 'S ne if "save: scalar as filename expected!\n" . break then
  "Saving workspace to " over ": " 3 compress "" join .
  '> swap open '_save_destination set
  _save_destination fout
  wlist vlist append uxplain drop
  STDOUT fout
  _save_destination close
  "done\n" .
;

# Read a file (the filename is expected to be in TOS) and create an array
# containing one record of this file per element.
: slurp
  depth 1 < if "slurp: Not enough elements on stack!\n" panic then
  type 'S ne if "slurtp: Scalar as filename expected!\n" panic then
  '< swap open '__slurp_fh set __slurp_fh fin
  []
  do
    eof if break then
    read append
  loop
  __slurp_fh close
  STDIN fin
;

#=====================================================================
"Stk.." .

# Duplicate the two topmost elements on the stack.
: 2dup
  depth 2 < if "2dup: Not enough elements on stack!\n" panic then
  over over
;

# Remove all elements from stack.
: clear
  depth 0 > if depth compress drop then
;

# Generalized drop, TOS = depth.
: ndrop
  depth 1 < if "ndrop: Not enough elements on stack!\n" panic then
  type 'S ne if "ndrop: TOS is not scalar!\n" panic then
  compress drop
;

# Generalized over - it expects the position of the element to be picked
# at the TOS.
: pick
  depth 1 < if "pick: Not enough elements on stack!\n" panic then
  type 'S ne if "pick: TOS is not scalar!\n" panic then
```

```
  compress swap dup rot rot 1 compress append expand drop
;

# Generalized rot, TOS = depth.
: roll 1 _roll ;

# rotate the topmost 3 elements
: rot 3 1 _roll ;

#=======================================================================
"Struct.." .

# Append a scalar or a vector to another vector.
: append
  depth 2 < if "append: Not enough elements on stack!\n" panic then
  type 'S eq if 1 compress then
  type 'A ne if "append: Not an array!\n" panic then
  swap
  expand dup 2 + roll
  expand dup 2 + roll
  + compress
;

# Deep reduce - this word will reduce a nested structure to a single scalar
# regardless if its depth.
: dreduce
  over type 'A ne if "dreduce: TOS-1 is not an array!\n" panic then drop
  swap collapse swap reduce
;

# Extract an element from an array (subscript and remove combined) - TOS
# contains the element's number while TOS-1 contains the array.
: extract
  depth 2 < if "extract: Not enough elements on stack!\n" panic then
  type 'S ne if "extract: TOS is not scalar!\n" panic then
  over
  type 'A ne if "extract: TOS-1 is not an array!\n" panic then drop
  2dup 1 compress subscript rot rot remove swap expand drop
;

"\n" .
```

# Appendix C

# The mathematical library

```
#
#  mathlib.5 contains various word definitions to deal with sets,
# statistics or to plot data.
#
#  This module makes use of the following dresses:
#
# (c)       Complex numbers
# (m)       Matrix
# (p)       Polar coordinates
# (s)   Set
# (v)       Vector

"loading mathlib.5: " .

#=======================================================================
"Const.." .

# Useful constants:
: pi 1 1 atan2 4 * ;
: e   1 exp ;
: eps 1.e-10 ; # This is used in comparison operators etc.

#=======================================================================
"Basics.." .

# Calculate the factorial.
: !(*) iota 1 + '* reduce ;

# Absolute value.
: abs(*) dup 0 < if neg then ;

#  Very straight-forward and non-clever implementation of the choose
# operator -- it expects n k (TOS) on the stack:
: choose(*,*)
  2dup - 0 < if "choose: TOS must be <= TOS-1!\n" panic then
  2dup - ! rot ! rot ! rot * /
;

# Maximum of the two topmost stack elements:
: max(*,*) 2dup - 0 < if swap then drop ;

# Minimum of the two topmost stack elements:
```

```
: min(*,*) 2dup - 0 > if swap then drop ;

#======================================================================
"Set.." .

# distinct removes all elements from a set which occur more than once. As a
# side effect the resulting distinct set will be sorted.
: distinct(s)
  strip
  length 2 < if 's dress break then   # Nothing to do for an empty set.
  grade subscript                     # Sort the array representing the set.
  dup dup
  [-1] remove [undef] swap append     # Right shift the sorted array.
  == not select                       # Determine the duplicates, negate the
                                      # resulting boolean vector and select
  's dress                            # the unique elements.
;

# Return the intersection of two sets.
# The result is a set without duplicates.
: intersect(s,s)
  distinct strip swap distinct strip over in select 's dress
;

# subset expects two sets on the stack and tests if the one on the TOS is
# a subset of the one below it. In this case a 1 is left on the TOS,
# otherwise 0 is returned.
: subset(s,s) strip swap strip swap in '&& reduce ;

# Return the union of two sets without duplicates.
: union(s,s) strip swap strip append 's dress distinct ;

#======================================================================
"Stat.." .

# Calculate arithmetic mean of the elements of a vector.
: amean
  depth 1 < if "amean: Stack is empty!\n" panic then
  type 'A ne if "amean: TOS is not an array!\n" panic then
  length 0 == if drop 0 break then
  dup '+ reduce swap length swap drop /
;

# Compute the cubic mean of the elements of a vector:
# ((x ** 3 + x ** 3 + ... + x    ** 3) / n) ** (1 / 3)
#    0       1               n - 1
: cmean
  depth 1 < if "cmean: Stack is empty!\n" panic then
  type 'A ne if "cmean: TOS is not an array!\n" panic then
  length 0 == if drop 0 break then
  3 hoelder
;

# Compute the Pearson correlation coefficient:
: corr
  depth 2 < if "corr: Not enought elements on stack!\n" panic then
  type 'A ne if "corr: TOS is not an array!\n" panic then
  length '_x_len set
  swap
  type 'A ne if "corr: TOS-1 is not an array!\n" panic then
  length '_y_len set
  _x_len _y_len != if "corr: Array lengths differ!\n" panic then

  dup '+ reduce '_sy set
  dup dup * '+ reduce '_sy2 set
```

```
  swap
  dup '+ reduce '_sx set
  dup dup * '+ reduce '_sx2 set
  * '+ reduce '_sxy set
  _x_len _sxy * _sx _sy * -
  _x_len _sx2 * _sx dup * - sqrt
  _x_len _sy2 * _sy dup * - sqrt
  * /
;

# Compute the geometric mean of the elements of a vector:
# (x  * x  * ... * x      ) ** (1 / n)
#   0    1          n - 1
: gmean
  depth 1 < if "gmean: Stack is empty!\n" panic then
  type 'A ne if "gmean: TOS is not an array!\n" panic then
  length 0 == if drop 0 break then
  length swap '* reduce swap 1 swap / **
;

# Compute the harmonic mean of the elements of a vector:
# n / (1 / x + 1 / x  + ... + 1 / x      )
#          0       1              n - 1
: hmean
  depth 1 < if "hmean: Stack is empty!\n" panic then
  type 'A ne if "hmean: TOS is not an array!\n" panic then
  length 0 == if drop 0 break then
  -1 hoelder
;

# Compute the hoelder mean of the elements of a vector:
# ((x ** k + x ** k + ... + x      ** k) / n) ** (1 / k)
#    0        1              n - 1
: hoelder
  depth 2 <
    if "hoelder: This word needs two words on the stack!\n" panic then
  type 'S ne if "hoelder: TOS is no a scalar!\n"    panic then
  swap type 'A ne if "hoelder: TOS-1 is not an array!\n" panic then swap
  over length swap drop 0 == if drop drop 0 break then
  swap length swap 2 pick ** '+ reduce swap / 1 rot / **
;

# Compute the median of the elements of a vector. The result is computed
# like this for a sorted vector:
#                 / x                for an odd number of elements
#                 !  (n + 1) / 2
#       x       = <
#        median   ! (x      + x      ) / 2 for an even number of elts
#                 \   n / 2    n / 2 + 1
#
: median
  depth 1 < if "median: Stack is empty!\n" panic then
  type 'A ne if "median: TOS is not an array!\n" panic then
  length 0 == if drop 0 break then
  grade subscript  # Sort the vector elements.
  length dup 2 %
  0 == if              # The vector has an even number of elements.
    2 / 2dup
    1 - 1 compress subscript expand drop
    rot rot
    1 compress subscript expand drop
    + 2 /
  else                 # Odd number of vector elements.
    1 + 2 / 1 - 1 compress subscript expand drop
  then
```

```
;

# Compute the quadratic mean of the elements of a vector:
# sqrt((x ** 2 + x ** 2 + ... + x     ** 2) / n)
#        0         1                n - 1
: qmean
  depth 1 < if "qmean: Stack is empty!\n" panic then
  type 'A ne if "qmean: TOS is not an array!\n" panic then
  length 0 == if drop 0 break then
  2 hoelder
;


#=======================================================================
"Cplx.." . # Functionality for dealing with complex numbers.

# Overload 'abs to return the absolute value of a complex number.
: abs(c)
  strip 2 ** '+ reduce sqrt
;

# Overload 'neg to perform the complement operation on a complex number.
: neg(c)
  strip [1 -1] * 'c dress
;

# Addition of two complex numbers.
: +(c,c)
  strip swap strip + 'c dress
;

# Subtraction of two complex numbers.
: -(c,c)
  strip swap strip swap - 'c dress
;

# Multiplication of two complex numbers.
: *(c,c)
  strip swap strip swap
  [0 1 0 1] subscript swap [0 1 1 0] subscript
  * expand drop
  + rot rot - swap
  2 compress 'c dress
;

# Division of two complex numbers.
: /(c,c)
  strip dup 2 ** '+ reduce
  rot strip rot
  [0 1 0 1] subscript swap [0 1 1 0] subscript
  * reverse expand drop
  + rot rot swap - 2 pick / rot rot swap / swap
  2 compress 'c dress
;

# Return the real part of a complex number.
: re(c)
  strip expand drop drop
;

# Return the imaginary part of a complex number.
: im(c)
  strip expand drop swap drop
;

# Convert a complex number to a polar coordinate tuple.
```

```
: polar(c)
  strip dup
  2 ** '+ reduce sqrt # This yields the radius.
  swap
  dup [0 0] == '&& reduce
    if "Can not convert zero cplx to polar!\n" panic then
  expand drop atan2   # This yields phi.
  2 compress 'p dress # Make a polar coordinate tuple.
;

# Convert a polar coordinate tuple to a complex number.
: complex(p)
  strip expand drop 2dup
  cos * rot rot sin *
  2 compress 'c dress
;

# Overload == for comparing complex numbers.
: ==(c,c)
  strip swap strip - abs eps < '&& reduce
;

# Overload != for comparing complex numbers.
: !=(c,c)
  strip swap strip - abs eps > '|| reduce
;

#=========================================================================
"P.." .

# Overload == for polar tuples.
: ==(p,p)
  strip swap strip - abs eps < '&& reduce
;

# Overload != for polar tuples.
: !=(p,p)
  strip swap strip - abs eps > '|| reduce
;

#=========================================================================
"LA.." .

# Overload * for matrix-vector-multiplication.
: *(m,v)
  # Calculate the inner sum of a vector:
  : inner+(*) '+ reduce ;

  swap strip shape rot strip swap reshape *
  'inner+ apply
  'v dress
;

: *(m,m) # Overload '* for matrix-matrix-multiplication
  # If we multiply an n*m matrix (columns*rows) by an m*n matrix using the
  # already existing matrix-vector-multiplication, we will need m copies of
  # the first matrix. First of all, let us determine m (as a side effect,
  # this second matrix looses its matrix dress which will be useful soon):
  strip shape [1] subscript expand drop

  # Now we compress the first matrix into an array and reshape it so that
  # this array will contain m copies of the original matrix:
  rot 1 compress swap reshape

  # Now swap the two arrays
```

```
  swap

  # To apply the already existing matrix-vector-multiplication to these two
  # arrays we have to transpose the topmost two dimensional array and
  # transform it into a one dimensional array of vectors:
  : a2v(*) 'v dress ;
  strip 1 transpose 'a2v apply

  # Now let us apply the existing matrix-vector-multiplication:
  *

  # Since this yields a one dimensional array of vectors, we have to strip
  # the array elements and dress the array itself as being a matrix:
  : v2a(v) strip ;
  'v2a apply

  # The result is still transposed, so perform another transposition and
  # dress it:
  1 transpose 'm dress
;

# Create a identity matrix
: idmatrix(*) iota dup '== outer 'm dress ;

#=======================================================================
"Graph.." .

# gplot plots a graph based on the elements of a single, one dimensional
# array (the name reflects the fact that only the y-coordinates are fed
# into gnuplot).
: gplot
  # _gplot_write_data is a unary word to be used with apply to write the
  # data to be plotted to the gnuplot scratch data file.
  : _gplot_write_data(*) . ;

  depth 1 < if "gplot: Stack is empty!\n" panic then
  type 'A ne if "gplot: TOS is not an array!\n" panic then

  "_5_gplot.data" '__gplot_data_name set
  "_5_gplot.cmd"  '__gplot_cmd_name  set

  '> __gplot_data_name open '__gplot_fh set
  __gplot_fh fout
  '_gplot_write_data apply drop
  __gplot_fh close

  '> __gplot_cmd_name open '__gplot_fh set
  __gplot_fh fout
  "set key off\n" .
  "plot \"" __gplot_data_name "\" with lines\n" 3 compress "" join .
  __gplot_fh close

  STDOUT fout

  'gnuplot __gplot_cmd_name 2 compress " " join system drop
  __gplot_data_name unlink
  __gplot_cmd_name  unlink
;

#=======================================================================
"Trig.." .

: tan dup sin swap cos / ;

#=======================================================================
```

```
"NT.." .

# Places 1 on TOS if TOS was prime, 0 otherwise.
: prime(*)
  type 'S ne if "prime: TOS is not scalar!\n" panic then
  dup 1 == if drop 0 then
  dup 4 < if break then
  dup sqrt 2 / int iota 1 + 2 * 1 + [2] swap append % '&& reduce
;

# Return the gcd of two integers
: gcd(*,*)
  do
    2dup 0 > swap 0 > && not if break then
    2dup <= if
      over -
    else
      swap over - swap
    then
  loop
  dup 0 == if drop else swap drop then
;

#  Convert a hexadecimal number to decimal. The hex-number is an
# upper-case # string.
: h2d
  uc "0123456789ABCDEF" "" split swap "" split length iota reverse
  16 swap ** rot rot index collapse * '+ reduce
;

"\n" .
```

# Appendix D

# The Array::APX module

```
package Array::APX;

=pod

=head1 NAME

Array::APX - Array Programming eXtensions

=head1 VERSION

This document refers to version 0.6 of Array::APX

=head1 SYNOPSIS

    use strict;
    use warnings;

    use Array::APX qw(:all);

    # Create two vectors [0 1 2] and [3 4 5]:
    my $x = iota(3);
    my $y = iota(3) + 3;

    print "The first vector is  $x";
    print "The second vector is $y\n";

    # Add these vectors and print the result:
    print 'The sum of these two vectors is ', $x + $y, "\n";

    # Create a function to multiply two values:
    my $f = sub { $_[0] * $_[1] };

    # Create an outer product and print it:
    print "The outer product of these two vectors is\n", $x |$f| $y;

yields

    The first vector is  [    0    1    2 ]
    The second vector is [    3    4    5 ]

    The sum of these two vectors is [    3    5    7 ]

    The outer product of these two vectors is
```

129

```
[
   [    0    0    0 ]
   [    3    4    5 ]
   [    6    8   10 ]
]
```

=head1 DESCRIPTION

This module extends Perl-5 with some basic functionality commonly found in
array programming languages like APL, Lang5 etc. It is basically a wrapper
of Array::Deeputils and overloads quite some basic Perl operators in a way
that allows easy manipulation of nested data structures. These data
structures are basically blessed n-dimensional arrays that can be handled
in a way similar to APL or Lang5.

A nice example is the computation of a list of prime numbers using an
archetypical APL solution. The basic idea is this: Create an outer product
of two vectors [2 3 4 ... ]. The resulting matrix does not contain any
primes since every number is the product of at least two integers. Then
check for every number in the original vector [2 3 4 ... ] if it is a
member of this matrix. If not, it must be a prime number. The set
theoretic method 'in' returns a selection vector consisting of 0 and 1
values which can be used in a second step to select only the prime values
from the original vector. Using Array::APX this can be written in Perl
like this:

```
    use strict;
    use warnings;
    use Array::APX qw(:all);

    my $f = sub { $_[0] * $_[1] }; # We need an outer product
    my $x;

    print $x->select(!($x = iota(199) + 2)->in($x |$f| $x));
```

How does this work? First a vector [2 3 4 ... 100] is created:

```
    $x = iota(99) + 2
```

This vector is then used to create an outer product (basically a
multiplication table without the 1-column/row:

```
    my $f = sub { $_[0] * $_[1] }; # We need an outer product
    ... $x |$f| $x ...
```

The |-operator is used here as the generalized outer-'product'-operator
(if applied to two APX data structures it would act as the bitwise binary
or) - it expects a function reference like $f in the example above. Thus
it is possible to create any outer 'products' - not necessarily based on
multiplication only.
Using the vector stored in $x and this two dimensional matrix, the
in-method is used to derive a boolean vector that contains a 1 at every
place corresponding to an element on the left hand operand that is
contained in the right hand operand. This boolean vector is then inverted
using the overloaded !-operator:

```
  !($x = iota(99) + 2)->in($x |$f| $x)
```

Using the select-method this boolean vector is used to select the elements
corresponding to places marked with 1 from the original vector $x thus
yielding a vector of prime numbers between 2 and 100:

```
    print $x->select(!($x = iota(199) + 2)->in($x |$f| $x));
```

=cut

```perl
use strict;
use warnings;

require Exporter;
our @ISA         = qw(Exporter);
our @EXPORT_OK   = qw(dress iota);
our %EXPORT_TAGS = ( 'all' => [ @EXPORT_OK ] );

our $VERSION = 0.6;

use Data::Dumper;
#use Array::DeepUtils qw(:all);
use Array::DeepUtils;
use Carp;

# The following operators will be generated automatically:
my %binary_operators = (
    '+'  => 'add',
    '*'  => 'multiply',
    '-'  => 'subtract',
    '%'  => 'mod',
    '**' => 'power',
    '&'  => 'bitwise_and',
    '^'  => 'bitwise_xor',
);

# Overload everything defined in %binary_operators:
eval "use overload '$_' => '$binary_operators{$_}';"
    for keys(%binary_operators);

# Binary operators with trick (0 instead of '' or undef) - these will be
# generated automatically, too:
my %special_binary_operators = (
    '==' => 'numeric_equal',
    '!=' => 'numeric_not_equal',
    '<'  => 'numeric_less_than',
    '<=' => 'numeric_less_or_equal',
    '>'  => 'numeric_greater_than',
    '>=' => 'numeric_greater_or_equal',
    'eq' => 'string_equal',
    'ne' => 'string_not_equal',
    'lt' => 'string_less_than',
    'le' => 'string_less_or_equal',
    'gt' => 'string_greater_than',
    'ge' => 'string_greater_or_equal',
);

# Overload everything defined in %special_binary_operatos:
eval "use overload '$_' => '$special_binary_operators{$_}';"
    for keys(%special_binary_operators);

# All other overloads are here:
use overload (
# Unary operators:
    '!' => 'not',
# Non-standard operators:
    '|'  => 'outer',  # This also implements the bitwise binary 'or'!
    '/'  => 'reduce', # This also implements the binary division operator!
    'x'  => 'scan',
    '""' => '_stringify',
);

########################################################################
# Overloading unary operators:
```

```
#######################################################################

=head1 Overloaded unary operators

Overloaded unary operators are automatically applied to all elements of
a (nested) APX data structure. The following operators are currently
available: !

=cut

sub not # Not, mapped to '!'.
{
    my $data = [@{$_[0]}];
    Array::DeepUtils::unary($data, sub { return 0+ !$_[0] });
    return bless $data;
}

#######################################################################
# Overloading binary operators:
#######################################################################

=head1 Overloaded binary operators

In general all overloaded binary operators are automatically applied in an
element wise fashion to all (corresponding) elements of APX data
structures.

The following operators are currently available and do what one would
expect:

=head2 +,-,*,/,%,**,|,&,^,==,!=,<,>,<=,>=,eq,ne,le,lt,ge,gt

These operators implement addition, subtraction, multiplication, division,
modulus, power, bitwise or / and /xor, numerical equal/not equal,
numerical less than, numerical greater than, numerical less or equal,
numerical greater or equal, string equal, string not equal, string less
than, string less or equal, string greater than, string greater or equal

=cut

# Overload basic binary operators:
eval ('
    sub ' . $binary_operators{$_} . '
    {
        my ($self, $other, $swap) = @_;
        my $result = ref($other) ? [@$other] : [$other];
        ($self, $result) = ($result, [@$self]) if $swap;
        _binary([@$self], $result, sub { $_[0] ' . $_ . ' $_[1] }, 1);
        return bless $result;
    }
') for keys(%binary_operators);

eval ('
    sub ' . $special_binary_operators{$_} . '
    {
        my ($self, $other, $swap) = @_;
        my $result = ref($other) ? [@$other] : [$other];
        ($self, $result) = ($result, [@$self]) if $swap;
        _binary([@$self], $result, sub { 0+ ($_[0] ' . $_ . ' $_[1]) }, 1);
        return bless $result;
    }
') for keys(%special_binary_operators);

=head2 Generalized outer products
```

A basic function in every array programming language is an operator to
create generalized outer products of two vectors. This generalized outer
product operator consists of a function pointer that is enclosed in two
'|' (cf. the prime number example at the beginning of this documentation).
Given two APX vectors a traditional outer product can be created like
this:

```
use strict;
use warnings;
use Array::APX qw(:all);

my $f = sub { $_[0] * $_[1] };
my $x = iota(10) + 1;
print $x |$f| $x;
```

This short program yields the following output:

```
[
  [   1   2   3   4   5   6   7   8   9   10 ]
  [   2   4   6   8  10  12  14  16  18   20 ]
  [   3   6   9  12  15  18  21  24  27   30 ]
  [   4   8  12  16  20  24  28  32  36   40 ]
  [   5  10  15  20  25  30  35  40  45   50 ]
  [   6  12  18  24  30  36  42  48  54   60 ]
  [   7  14  21  28  35  42  49  56  63   70 ]
  [   8  16  24  32  40  48  56  64  72   80 ]
  [   9  18  27  36  45  54  63  72  81   90 ]
  [  10  20  30  40  50  60  70  80  90  100 ]
]
```

```
=cut

# Create a generalized outer 'product' based on a function reference.
# In addition to that the |-operator which is overloaded here can also act
# as binary 'or' if applied to two APX structures.
my @_outer_stack;
sub outer
{
    my ($left, $right) = @_;

    if ((ref($left) eq __PACKAGE__ and ref($right) eq __PACKAGE__) or
        (ref($left) eq __PACKAGE__ and defined($right) and !ref($right))
       ) # Binary or
    {
        my ($self, $other) = @_;
        my $result = ref($right) ? [@$right] : [$right];
        Array::DeepUtils::binary([@$left], $result,
                                  sub {$_[0] | $_[1]}, 1);
        return bless $result;
    }
    # If the right side argument is a reference to a subroutine we are at
    # the initial stage of a |...|-operator and have to rememeber the
    # function to be used as well as the left hand operator:
    elsif (ref($left) eq __PACKAGE__ and ref($right) eq 'CODE')
    {
        my %outer;
        $outer{left}     = $left;  # APX object
        $outer{operator} = $right; # Reference to a subroutine
        push @_outer_stack, \%outer;
        return;
    }
    elsif (ref($left) eq __PACKAGE__ and !defined($right))
    {   # Second phase of applying the |...|-operator:
        my $info = pop @_outer_stack;
        my ($a1, $a2) = ([@{$info->{left}}], [@{$left}]);
```

```
        my @result;

        for my $i ( 0 .. @$a1 - 1 )
        {
            for my $j ( 0 .. @$a2 - 1 )
            {
                my $value = $a2->[$j];
                _binary($a1->[$i], $value, $info->{operator}));
                $result[$i][$j] = $value;
            }
        }

        return bless \@result;
    }

    croak 'outer: Strange parametertypes: >>', ref($left),
        '<< and >>', ref($right), '<<';
}
```

=head2 The reduce operator /

The operator / acts as the reduce operator if applied to a reference to a
subroutine as its left argument and an APX structure as its right element:

```
    use strict;
    use warnings;
    use Array::APX qw(:all);

    my $x = iota(100) + 1;
    my $f = sub { $_[0] + $_[1] };

    print $f/ $x, "\n";
```

calculates the sum of all integers between 1 and 100 (without using Gauss'
summation formula just by repeated addition). The combined operator

```
    $f/
```

applies the function referenced by $f between each two successive elements
of the APX structure on the right hand side of the operator.

=cut

```
sub reduce
{
    my ($left, $right, $swap) = @_;

    if (ref($left) eq __PACKAGE__ and ref($right) ne 'CODE') # Binary div.
    {
        my $result = ref($right) ? [@$right] : [$right];
        ($left, $result) = ($result, [@$left]) if $swap;
        _binary([@$left], $result, sub { $_[0] / $_[1] }, 1);
        return bless $result;
    }
    elsif (ref($_[0]) eq __PACKAGE__ and ref($_[1]) eq 'CODE') # reduce
    {
        my $result = shift @$left;
        for my $element (@$left)
        {
            eval { _binary($element, $result, $right); };
            croak "reduce: Error while applying reduce: $@\n" if $@;
        }

        return $result;
    }
```

```
    croak 'outer: Strange parametertypes: ', ref($_[0]), ' and ',
        ref($_[0]);
}
```

=head2 The scan operator x

The scan-operator works like the \-operator in APL - it applies a binary
function to all successive elements of an array but accumulates the
results gathered along the way. The following example creates a vector of
the partial sums of 0, 0 and 1, 0 and 1 and 2, 0 and 1 and 2 and 3 etc.:

```
    $f = sub { $_[0] + $_[1] };
    $x = $f x iota(10);
    print $x;
```

This code snippet yields the following result:

```
    [   0   1   3   6   10   15   21   28   36   45 ]
```

=cut

```
sub scan
{
    my ($argument, $function, $swap) = @_;

    croak "scan operator: Wrong sequence of function and argument!\n"
        unless $swap;

    croak "scan operator: No function reference found!\n"
        if ref($function) ne 'CODE';

    my @result;
    push @result, (my $last_value = shift @$argument);
    for my $element (@$argument)
    {
        _binary($element, $last_value, $function);
        push @result, $last_value;
    }

    return bless \@result;
}


########################################################################
# Exported functions:
########################################################################

=head1 Exported functions

=head2 dress
```

This function expects an array reference and converts it into an APX
objects. This is useful if nested data structures that have been created
outside of the APX framework are to be processed using the APX array
processing capabilities.

```
    use strict;
    use warnings;
    use Array::APX qw(:all);

    my $array = [[1, 2], [3, 4]];
    my $x = dress($array);
    print "Structure:\n$x";
```

yields the following output:

```
    Structure:
    [
      [    1    2 ]
      [    3    4 ]
    ]
```

=cut

```perl
sub dress # Transform a plain vanilla Perl array into an APX object.
{
    my ($value) = @_;
    croak "Can't dress a non-reference!" if ref($value) ne 'ARRAY';
    return bless $value;
}
```

=head2 iota

This function expects a positive integer value as its argument and returns
an APX vector with unit stride, starting with 0 and containing as many
elements as specified by the argument:

```perl
    use strict;
    use warnings;
    use Array::APX qw(:all);

    my $x = iota(10);
    print "Structure:\n$x";
```

yields

```
    Structure:
    [    0    1    2    3    4    5    6    7    8    9 ]
```

=cut

```perl
# Create a unit stride vector starting at 0:
sub iota
{
    my ($argument) = @_;

    croak "iota: Argument is not a positive integer >>$argument<<\n"
        if $argument !~ /^[+]?\d+$/;

    return bless [ 0 .. $_[0] - 1 ];
}
```

```
##########################################################################
# APX-methods:
##########################################################################
```

=head1 APX-methods

=head2 collapse

To convert an n-dimensional APX-structure into a one dimensional
structure, the collapse-method is used:

```perl
    use strict;
    use warnings;

    use Array::APX qw(:all);

    print dress([[1, 2], [3, 4]])->collapse();
```

yields

```
    [    1    2    3    4 ]
```

=cut

```
sub collapse { return bless Array::DeepUtils::collapse([@{$_[0]}]); }
```

=head2 grade

The grade-method returns an index vector that can be used to sort the
elements of the object, grade was applied to. For example

```
    print dress([3, 1, 4, 1, 5, 9, 2, 6, 5, 3, 5])->grade();
```

yields

```
    [    3    1    6    9    0    2    8    4    10    7    5 ]
```

So to sort the elements of the original object, the subscript-method could
be applied with this vector as its argument.

=cut

```
sub grade
{
    my ($data) = @_;

    my %h = map { $_ => $data->[$_] } 0 .. @$data - 1;

    return bless [ sort { $h{$a} <=> $h{$b} } keys %h ];
}
```

=head2 in

This implements the set theoretic 'in'-function. It checks which elements
of its left operand data structure are elements of the right hand data
structure and returns a boolean vector that contains a 1 at corresponding
locations of the left side operand that are elements of the right side
operand.

```
    use strict;
    use warnings;
    use Array::APX qw(:all);

    my $x = iota(10);
    my $y = dress([5, 11, 3, 17, 2]);
    print "Boolean vector:\n", $y->in($x);
```

yields

```
    Boolean vector:
    [    1    0    1    0    1 ]
```

Please note that the in-method operates on a one dimensional APX-object
while its argument can be of any dimension >= 1.

=cut

```
# Set function 'in':
sub in
{
    my ($what, $where) = @_;

    croak 'in: argument is not an APX-object: ', ref($where), "\n"
```

```
        unless ref($where) eq __PACKAGE__;

    my @result;
    push (@result, _is_in($_, $where)) for (@$what);
    return bless \@result;
}

sub int
{
    my $data = [@{$_[0]}];
    Array::DeepUtils::unary($data, sub { return int($_[0]) });
    return bless $data;
}
```

=head2 index

The index-method returns an index vector containing the indices of the
elements of the object it was applied to with respect to its argument
which must be an APX-object, too. Thus

```
    print dress([[1,3], [4,5]])->index(dress([[1,2,3], [4,5,6], [7,8,9]]));
```

yields

```
    [
      [
        [    0    0 ]
        [    0    2 ]
      ]
      [
        [    1    0 ]
        [    1    1 ]
      ]
    ]
```

=cut

```
sub index
{
    my ($a, $b) = @_;

    croak 'index: argument is not an APX-object: ', ref($b), "\n"
        unless ref($b) eq __PACKAGE__;

    return bless Array::DeepUtils::idx([@$a], [@$b]);
}
```

=head2 remove

The remove-method removes elements from an APX-object controlled by an
index vector supplied as its argument (which must be an APX-object,
too):

```
    print iota(10)->remove(dress([1, 3, 5]));
```

yields

```
    [    0    2    4    6    7    8    9 ]
```

=cut

```
sub remove
{
    my ($a, $b) = @_;
```

```
    croak 'remove: argument is not an APX-object: ', ref($b), "\n"
        unless ref($b) eq __PACKAGE__;

    $a = [@$a];
    Array::DeepUtils::remove($a, [@$b]);
    return bless $a;
}
```

=head2 reverse

The reverse-method reverses the sequence of elements in an APX-object, thus

```
    print iota(5)->reverse();
```

yields

```
    [    4    3    2    1    0 ]
```

=cut

```
sub reverse { return bless [reverse(@{$_[0]})]; }
```

=head2 rho

The reshape-method has fulfills a twofold function: If called without any
argument it returns an APX-object describing the structure of the object
it was applied to. If called with an APX-object as its parameter, the
rho-method restructures the object it was applied to according to the
dimension values specified in the parameter (please note that rho will
reread values from the object it was applied to if there are not enough
to fill the destination structure). The following code example shows both
usages of rho:

```
    use strict;
    use warnings;

    use Array::APX qw(:all);

    my $x = iota(9);
    my $y = dress([3, 3]);

    print "Data rearranged as 3-times-3-matrix:\n", my $z = $x->rho($y);
    print 'Dimensionvector of this result: ', $z->rho();
```

This test program yields the following output:

```
    Data rearranged as 3-times-3-matrix:
    [
      [    0    1    2 ]
      [    3    4    5 ]
      [    6    7    8 ]
    ]
    Dimensionvector of this result: [    3    3 ]
```

=cut

```
sub rho
{
    my ($data, $control) = @_;

    if (!defined($control)) # Return a structure object
    {
        return bless Array::DeepUtils::shape([@$data]);
    }
```

```
    else
    {
        croak "rho: Control structure is not an APX-object!"
            if ref($control) ne __PACKAGE__;

        return bless Array::DeepUtils::reshape([@$data], [@$control]);
    }
}
```

=head2 rotate

rotate rotates an APX-structure along several axes. The following example
shows the rotation of a two dimensional data structure along its x- and
y-axes by +1 and -1 positions respecitively:

```
    print dress([[1, 2, 3], [4, 5, 6], [7, 8, 9]])->rotate(dress([1, -1]));
```

The result of this rotation is thus

```
    [
      [    8    9    7 ]
      [    2    3    1 ]
      [    5    6    4 ]
    ]
```

=cut

```
sub rotate
{
    my ($a, $b) = @_;

    croak 'rotate: argument is not an APX-object: ', ref($b), "\n"
        unless ref($b) eq __PACKAGE__;

    return bless Array::DeepUtils::rotate([@$a], [@$b]);
}
```

=head2 scatter

The scatter-method is the inverse of subscript. While subscript selects
values from an APX-object, controlled by an index vector, scatter creates
a new data structure with elements read from the APX-object it was applied
to and their positions controlled by an index vector. The following
example shows the use of scatter:

```
    print (iota(7) + 1)->scatter(dress([[0, ,0], [0, 1], [1, 0], [1, 1]]));
```

yields

```
    [
      [    1    2 ]
      [    3    4 ]
    ]
```

=cut

```
sub scatter
{
    my ($a, $b) = @_;

    croak 'scatter: argument is not an APX-object: ', ref($b), "\n"
        unless ref($b) eq __PACKAGE__;

    return bless Array::DeepUtils::scatter([@$a], [@$b]);
}
```

=head2 select

The select-method is applied to a boolean vector and selects those
elements from its argument vector that correspond to places containing
a true value in the boolean vector. Thus

```
    use strict;
    use warnings;
    use Array::APX qw(:all);

    my $x = iota(10) + 1;
    my $s = dress([0, 1, 1, 0, 1, 0, 1]);

    print $x->select($s);
```

yields

```
    [    2    3    5    7 ]
```

Please note that select works along the first dimension of the APX-object
it is applied to and expects a one dimensional APX-objects as its argument.

=cut

```
sub select
{
    my ($data, $control) = @_;

    croak 'select: argument is not an APX-object: ', ref($control), "\n"
        unless ref($control) eq __PACKAGE__;

    my @result;
    for my $i ( 0 .. @$control - 1 )
    {
        push (@result, $data->[$i]) if $control->[$i];
    }

    return bless \@result;
}
```

=head2 slice

slice extracts part of a nested data structure controlled by a coordinate
vector as the following example shows:

```
  print (iota(9) + 1)->rho(dress([3, 3]))->slice(dress([[1, 0], [2, 1]]));
```

yields

```
    [
      [    4    5 ]
      [    7    8 ]
    ]
```

=cut

```
sub slice
{
    my ($data, $control) = @_;

    croak 'slice: argument is not an APX-object: ', ref($control), "\n"
        unless ref($control) eq __PACKAGE__;

    return bless Array::DeepUtils::dcopy([@$data], [@$control]);
```

```
}
```

=head2 strip

strip is the inverse function to dress() - it is applied to an APX data
structure and returns a plain vanilla Perl array:

```
    use strict;
    use warnings;
    use Array::APX qw(:all);
    use Data::Dumper;

    my $x = iota(3);
    print Dumper($x->strip);
```

yields

```
    $VAR1 = [
              0,
              1,
              2
            ];
```

=cut

```
sub strip { return [@{$_[0]}]; }
```

=head2 subscript

The subscript-method retrieves values from a nested APX-data structure
controlled by an index vector (an APX-object, too) as the following
simple example shows:

```
    print (iota(9) + 1)->rho(dress([3, 3]))->subscript(dress([1]));
```

returns the element with the index 1 from a two dimensional data
structure that contains the values 1 to 9 yielding:

```
    [
      [    4    5    6 ]
    ]
```

=cut

```
sub subscript
{
    my ($data, $control) = @_;

    croak 'subscript: arg is not an APX-object: ', ref($control), "\n"
        unless ref($control) eq __PACKAGE__;

    return bless Array::DeepUtils::subscript([@$data], [@$control]);
}
```

=head2 transpose

transpose is used to transpose a nested APX-structure along any of its
axes. In the easiest two dimensional case this corresponds to the
traditional matrix transposition, thus

```
    print (iota(9) + 1)->rho(dress([3, 3]))->transpose(1);
```

yields

```
    [
```

```
        [   1    4    7 ]
        [   2    5    8 ]
        [   3    6    9 ]
    ]

=cut

sub transpose
{
    my ($data, $control) = @_;

    croak "transpose: argument is not an integer: >>$control<<\n"
        if $control !~ /^[+-]?\d+/;

    return bless Array::DeepUtils::transpose([@$data], $control);
}

#######################################################################
# Support functions - not to be exported (these are mostly copied from
# Lang5).
#######################################################################

# Apply a binary word to a nested data structure.
sub _binary {
    my $func = $_[2];

    # both operands not array refs -> exec and early return
    if ( ref($_[0]) ne 'ARRAY' and ref($_[1]) ne 'ARRAY' ) {
        $_[1] = $func->($_[0], $_[1]);
        return 1;
    }

    # no eval because _binary will be called in an eval {}
    Array::DeepUtils::binary($_[0], $_[1], $func);

    return 1;
}

# Implements '.'; dump a scalar or structure to text.
sub _stringify {
    my($element) = @_;
    $element = [@$element];

    # shortcut for simple scalars
    if ( !ref($element) or ref($element) eq 'Lang5::String' ) {
      $element = 'undef' unless defined $element;
      $element .= "\n"
        if $element =~ /^([+-]?)(?=\d|\.\d)\d*(\.\d*)?([Ee]([+-]?\d+))?$/;
      return $element;
    }

    my $indent = 2;
    my @estack = ( $element );
    my @istack = ( 0 );

    my $txt = '';

    while ( @estack ) {

        my $e = $estack[-1];
        my $i = $istack[-1];

        # new array: output opening bracket
        if ( $i == 0 ) {
            if ( $txt ) {
```

```
                $txt .= "\n";
                $txt .= ' ' x ( $indent * ( @istack - 1 ) );
            }
            $txt .= '[';
        }

        if ( $i <= $#$e   ) {
            # push next reference and a new index onto stacks
            if ( ref($e->[$i]) and ref($e->[$i]) ne 'Lang5::String' ) {
                push @estack, $e->[$i];
                push @istack, 0;
                next;
            }

            # output element
            if ( $txt =~ /\]$/ ) {
                $txt .= "\n";
                $txt .= ' ' x ( $indent * @istack );
            } else {
                $txt .= ' ';
            }
            $txt .= defined($e->[$i]) ? sprintf("%4s", $e->[$i]) : 'undef';
        }

        # after last item, close arrays
        # on an own line and indent next line
        if ( $i >= $#$e ) {

            my($ltxt) = $txt =~ /(?:\A|\n)([^\n]*?)$/;

            #  The current text should not end in a closing bracket as it
            # would if we had typed an array and it should not end in a
            # parenthesis as it would if we typed an array with an object
            # type .
            if ( $ltxt =~ /\[/ and $ltxt !~ /\]|\)$/ ) {
                $txt .= ' ';
            } else {
                $txt .= "\n";
                $txt .= ' ' x ( $indent * ( @istack - 1 ) );
            }
            $txt .= ']';

            # Did we print an element that had an object type set?
            my $last_type = ref(pop @estack);
            $txt .= "($last_type)"
                if $last_type
                   and
                   $last_type ne 'ARRAY'
                   and
                   $last_type ne 'Lang5::String';
            pop @istack;
        }

        $istack[-1]++
            if @istack;
    }

    $txt .= "\n" unless $txt =~ /\n$/;

    return $txt;
}

# Return 1 if a scalar element is found in a structure (set operation in).
sub _is_in
{
```

```
    my($el, $data) = @_;

    for my $d ( @$data )
    {
        if ( ref($d) eq 'ARRAY' )
        {
            return 1 if _is_in($el, $d);
        }

        return 1 if $el eq $d;
    }

    return 0;
}
```

=head1 SEE ALSO

Array::APX relies mainly on Array::Deeputils which, in turn, was developed
for the interpreter of the array programming language Lang5. The source of
Array::Deeputils is maintained in the source repository of Lang. In
addition to that Array::APX borrows some basic functions of the Lang5
interpreter itself, too.

=head2 Links

=over

=item *

L<The lang5 Home Page|http://lang5.sf.net/>.

=back

=head1 AUTHOR

Bernd Ulmann <lt>ulmann@vaxman.de<gt>

Thomas Kratz <lt>tomk@cpan.org<gt>

=head1 COPYRIGHT

Copyright (C) 2012 by Bernd Ulmann, Thomas Kratz

This library is free software; you can redistribute it and/or
modify it under the same terms as Perl itself, either Perl version
5.8.8 or, at your option, any later version of Perl 5 you may
have available.

=cut

1;

# Appendix E

# Solutions to selected exercises

---

**Solution 3:**

1. lang5> 1.25 2 / 2 ** pi * .
   1.22718463030851

2. lang5> 2 3 + 5 + 8 + 13 + .
   31
   lang5> 2 3 5 8 13 + + + + .
   31

   Using a more sophisticated function, this problem
   could be solved like this:

   lang5> [2 3 5 8 13] '+ reduce .
   31

---

**Solution 4:**

1. lang5> [[1 2 3] [4 5 6] [7 8 9]]
   lang5> [[7 6 2] [1 9 5] [3 8 4]] + .
   [
     [    8      8      5   ]
     [    5     14     11   ]
     [   10     16     13   ]
   ]

---

```
2.  lang5> [[1 2 3] [4 5 6] [7 8 9]] 1 - .
    [
       [   0    1    2  ]
       [   3    4    5  ]
       [   6    7    8  ]
    ]
```

### Solution 5:

```
lang5> 5 do dup . 1 - dup 1 < if break then loop
5
4
3
2
1
```

### Solution 6:

: square dup * ; applied to a vector returns a vector of the same size with the squares of the elements of the original vector. This is due to the fact that although the word square itself is *not* applied in an element-wise fashion to the vector, the dup duplicates the vector as a whole and the multiplication operator * is then applied to the elements of the resulting two identical vectors.

### Solution 7:

```
lang5> : binary_print(*,*) . . "------\n" . ;
lang5> [1 2 3] 1 binary_print
1
1
------
1
2
------
1
3
------
```

Since binary_print is a binary word, the interpreter automatically expands the smaller data structure (the scalar in this case) to match the structure of the larger argument (the vector). So binary_print is implicitly applied to two vectors [1 2 3] and [1 1 1] respectively.

### Solution 8:

```
lang5> : square dup * ;
lang5> [1 2 3 4] 'vector set
lang5> vector square .
[    1    4    9    16  ]
```

### Solution 9:

```
: *(baz,baz)
  strip swap strip
  * -1 *
  'baz dress
;

[1 2 3](baz) [4 5 6](baz) * .
```

### Solution 10:

```
lang5> : twodup over over ;
lang5> 1 2 twodup .s
vvvvvvvvvv Begin of stack listing vvvvvvvvvv
Stack contents (TOS at bottom):
1
2
1
2
^^^^^^^^^^ End of stack listing ^^^^^^^^^^
```

### Solution 11:

```
lang5> : twodup 1 pick 1 pick ;
```

```
lang5> 1 2 twodup .s
vvvvvvvvvv Begin of stack listing vvvvvvvvvv
Stack contents (TOS at bottom):
1
2
1
2
^^^^^^^^^^ End of stack listing ^^^^^^^^^^
```

### Solution 12:

```
: myroll 1 _roll ;
```

### Solution 13:

```
lang5> : myswap over rot drop ;
lang5> 1 2 myswap . .
1
2
```

### Solution 14:

```
lang5> : mydreduce swap collapse swap reduce ;
lang5> [[1 2] [3 4]] '+ mydreduce .
10
```

### Solution 15:

```
lang5> : myfactorial iota 1 + '* reduce ;
lang5> 5 myfactorial .
120
```

### Solution 16:

To create an $n$ times $n$ identity matrix, a vector looking like [1 0 ...0] containing $n+1$ elements is created. This vector is then reshaped into a $n$ times $n$ matrix. Since

reshape reads the source data structure over and over
again to fill the destination structure, this will eventually
produce the identity matrix.

```
: identity_matrix
  dup
  1 + iota 0 ==
  swap dup 2 compress
  reshape
;

3 identity_matrix .
```

### Solution 17:

```
lang5> 10 iota 2 * 1 + '+ spread .
[    1     4     9    16    25    36    49
     64    81   100   ]
```

### Solution 18:

```
: compute_mean_grade
  #  Define a support word to get rid of
  # the student names:
  : get_second_element(*) '; split 0 remove ;

  slurp                       # Read in file
  0 remove                    # Remove header
  get_second_element collapse # Create a one-
                              # dimensional
                              # structure
  amean                       # Compute the mean
;

'grades.dat compute_mean_grade .
```

### Solution 19:

```
lang5> : largest_only over < select ;
```

```
lang5> [1 2 3] [0 2 2] largest_only .
[    1    3   ]
```

**Solution 20:**

```
lang5> : myamean length swap '+ reduce swap / ;
lang5> [1 2 3 4] myamean .
2.5
```

**Solution 21:**

```
lang5> : setmax 'max spread length 1 - extract ;
lang5> [3 1 4 1 5 9 2 6 5 3 5](s) setmax .
9
```

**Solution 22:**

```
lang5> : p_list 1 - iota 2 + dup prime select ;
lang5> 100 p_list .
[    2     3     5     7    11    13    17    19
    23    29    31    37    41    43    47    53
    59    61    67    71    73    79    83    89
    97   ]
```

**Solution 23:**

```
: better_sqrt
  dup abs sqrt
  swap 0 < if
    1 2 compress 'c dress
  then
;

2  better_sqrt .
-2 better_sqrt .
```

Another variant, yielding a complex number in every case
might look like this:

```
: better_sqrt
  dup abs sqrt
  swap 0 < 2 compress 'c dress
;

2  better_sqrt .
-2 better_sqrt .
```

### Solution 24:

```
: myprime(*)
  dup sqrt int 1 - dup rot swap reshape
  swap iota 2 +
  % 0 == '+ reduce
  0 ==
;

# Test the unary word myprime:
99 iota 2 + dup myprime select .
```

### Solution 29:

The values which are pushed to the local stack are automatically removed from the main stack. Thus, it is sufficient to work with references throughout since there is only one instance of these values and side-effects are impossible.

# Bibliography

[Adams et al. 2009] Jeanne C. Adams, Walter S. Brainerd, Richard A. Hendrickson, Richard E. Maine, Jeanne T. Martin, Brian T. Smith, *The Fortran 2003 Handbook*, Springer, 2009

[Burks et al. 1954] Arthur W. Burks, Don W. Warren, Jesse B. Wright, "An Analysis of a Logical Machine Using Parenthesis-Free Notation" in *Mathematical Tables and Other Aids to Computation*, Vol. 8, No. 46, Apr., 1954, pp. 53–57

[Dr. Dobb's Journal] Dr. Dobb's Journal, *C Tools*, Markt & Technik Verlag, 1986

[Falkoff et al. 1964] A. D. Falkoff, K. E. Iverson, E. H. Sussenguth, "A formal description of SYSTEM/360", in *IBM Systems Journal*, Vol 3, No. 3, 1964, pp. 198–261

[Gilman et al. 1970] Leonard Gilman, Allen J. Rose, *APL\360 an interactive approach*, John Wiley & Sons, Inc., 1970

[Holub 1985] Allen Holub, "Wie Compiler arbeiten", in [Dr. Dobb's Journal][pp. 153–167]

[Iverson 1962] Kenneth E. Iverson, *A Programming Language*, J. Wiley & Sons, New York, 1962

[Iverson 1963] Kenneth E. Iverson, "Notation as a Tool of Thought", in [N. N. 1981][pp. 105–128]

[Janko 1980] Wolfgang H. Janko, *APL 1 – Eine Einführung in die Elemente der Sprache und des Systems*, Athenaeum Verlag, Königstein/Ts., 1980

[LÜNEBURG 1993] HEINZ LÜNEBURG, *Leonardi Pisani Liber Abaci oder Lesevergnügen eines Mathematikers*, BI Wissenschaftsverlag, 1993

[MCDONNEL 1981] EUGENE E. MCDONNELL, "Introduction", in [N. N. 1981][p. 11–14]

[N. N. 1981] N. N., *A Source Book in APL*, APL PRESS, Palo Alto, 1981

[OUSTERHOUT 1998] JOHN K. OUSTERHOUT, "Scripting: Higher Level Programming for the 21st Century", in *IEEE Computer Magazine*, March 1998, see also http://www.eve.cmu.edu/~ganger/712. fall02/papers/scripting-computer98.ps, retrieved 01/14/2010

[PRECHELT 2010] LUTZ PRECHELT, *Are Scripting Languages Any Good? A Validation of Perl, Python, Rexx and Tcl against C, C++, and Java*, http://page.mi.fu-berlin. de/prechelt/Biblio/jccpprt2\_advances2003.pdf, retrieved 01/14/2010

[ULMANN 2012] BERND ULMANN, "Array programming for mere mortals", in *Proceedings YAPC::Europe 2012*, pp. 37–41

# Index